'I love the goal  our heart tanks conscience by the ... . and breathes new life into us with a pardon so scandalous that we cannot help but be changed". This is the kind of grace that makes disciples so love the Savior that they will give their lives for his glory.'

Bryan Chapell, Pastor Emeritus, Grace Presbyterian Church, Peoria, Illinois, President Emeritus, Covenant Theological Seminary

'Dane Ortlund … is a craftsman of prose, and more: he writes with theological discernment and an eye for heart application. To read this book is to have a surprising encounter with the Savior. Dane walks us through the four Gospels, highlighting Christ's astonishing words and actions — actions never more astonishing than at Calvary. More than anything, as I read these pages I was reminded of the Savior's stunning love for me and of his surprising grace — grace that is shockingly unmeasured, vast, and free.'

C. J. Mahaney, Senior Pastor, Sovereign Grace Church, Louisville, KY

'Dane Ortlund's *Surprised by Jesus* is a very helpful guide to a gospel-centered understanding of Christianity. Drawing from material gleaned from all four Gospels, Ortlund presents us with the compelling picture of subversive grace—so different from the pale and timid imitation of pallid, anemic religion. Read this book and soak in the gospel of grace!'

Josh Moody, Senior Pastor, College Church, Wheaton, author of *No Other Gospel*

'The world wants justice and, truth to tell, the church often wants that too. In this book, Dane Ortlund makes the case from the Gospels that what the church and the world to whom she witnesses needs is grace. Grace is counterintuitive, beyond price, and yet totally free. Left to ourselves, we hate it. We see it as demeaning. We regard it as witnessing to our moral corruption and weakness. Yet grace is God's way of salvation as revealed in the acts and sayings of Jesus in the four Gospels. This book is that strangest of things: the heartfelt rebuke which brings so much encouragement, freedom, and joy. Well worth reading.'

Carl R. Trueman, Professor, Grove City College, Pennsylvania

SURPRISED

by

JESUS

DANE ORTLUND

SURPRISED

by

JESUS

Subversive Grace in the Four Gospels

British Library Cataloguing in Publication Data
A record for this book is available from the British Library

ISBN: 978-1-78397-316-3

Designed by Jude May
Cover image © artbyjulie, Barks_japan | iStock

Printed in Denmark by Nørhaven

Evangelical Press, (EP Books), an imprint of 10Publishing
Unit C, Tomlinson Road, Leyland, PR25 2DY, England
Email: epbooks@10ofthose.com
Website: www.epbooks.org

For Dad,
who has convinced me of the truths of these pages
by word and, far more powerfully, by example.

Contents

PREFACE

THIS BOOK WAS birthed in a class taught on the four Gospels in the autumn of 2008 at Naperville Presbyterian Church and again, in a slightly different format, in 2009 at The Orchard Evangelical Free Church, both near Chicago, Illinois. I am indebted to the members of both classes for their enthusiasm and insights. The material has also been honed over the years through various other teaching and preaching opportunities, not least spending two weeks teaching the four Gospels at the Theological College of Central Africa in Ndola, Zambia.

This book was originally released under the title *Defiant Grace* in 2011; the present iteration, ten years on, retains much of the same material but it has been reworked and honed. It is a particular pleasure to me that the first venue of teaching this material, Naperville Presbyterian Church, is where I now serve, having been called to serve there pastorally in 2020.

Noting the seedbed of these reflections helps to explain their intended audience, emerging as they have in the context of the local church. This book is not written for the academy, though I have benefited from numerous scholars whose names only rarely surface in these pages. Nor is it aimed at Christian leaders, though the debt I owe certain leaders in today's church is beyond repayment. It is written for fellow everyday believers, or those investigating what Jesus was really all about — anyone interested in listening afresh to the heart of Christianity by listening to Jesus. If you want nothing to do with Christians or the church but are intrigued by Jesus himself, this book is for you. If, on the other hand, you consider yourself a Christian yet obedience has somehow come to feel like a tax paid to God (with the hope that you will have enough left over to live on), this book is equally for you.

I happily and gratefully acknowledge those teachers of mine who have informed the theological and personal background from which this book has emerged — some dead, others living; some by their writing, others by their friendship. Readers familiar with the ministries of Martin Luther, Jonathan Edwards, Adolf Schlatter, C. S. Lewis, Martyn Lloyd-Jones, Paul Tournier, Helmut Thielicke, Richard Bauckham, Brian Martin, and Ray Ortlund Jr. will gladly note the influence these gifts to the church have had on my own understanding of spiritual reality. This little book is theirs as much as mine. It is dedicated to the last-mentioned, my dad, who, in a hundred ways I recognize and a thousand I do not, has shown me the meaning and the beauty of the gospel.

I am grateful also to Brad Byrd and the team at 10Publishing.

Greater than my debt to any of these is that owed to my best friend and partner in life. Stacey not only read and improved every chapter, but continues to put up with and encourage me every day. For this and the countless other ways you brighten my life, thank you, sweetheart.

Dane Ortlund

Easter 2021

INTRODUCTION

JESUS IS SURPRISING. His coming fulfilled ancient prophecies, but not expectations. He shattered expectations.

Each of the four Gospel accounts in the Bible uniquely gives us a Jesus who turns upside down our intuitive anticipations of who he is and how following him works. Like a bad back that needs to return repeatedly to the chiropractor for straightening out, our understanding of Jesus needs to be straightened out over and over again as our poor spiritual posture throws our perception of him out of line — domesticating him and conforming him to our image, rather than transforming us into *his* image.

For the grace that comes to us in Jesus Christ is not measured. This grace refuses to allow itself to be tethered to our innate sense of fairness, reciprocity, and balancing of the scales. It is surprising.

Few have captured the surprise of grace better than the American Episcopalian priest and author Robert Farrar

Capon in his description of what the Protestant Reformers recovered five centuries ago. Reflecting on why Martin Luther refused to endorse forced celibacy on the priests, Capon wrote:

> The Reformation was a time when people went blind-staggering drunk because they had discovered, in the dusty basement of late medievalism, a whole cellarful of fifteen-hundred-year-old, 200-proof grace — of bottle after bottle of pure distillate of Scripture that would convince anyone that God saves us single-handed.[1]

The Reformation's rediscovery of grace is a discovery that must take place afresh, in kind if not in degree, in each generation. The church is always only a few generations away from losing the gospel. D. A. Carson recounts a memory both fascinating and frightening:

> I have heard a Mennonite leader assess his own movement in this way. One generation of Mennonites cherished the gospel and believed that the entailment of the gospel lay in certain social and political commitments. The next generation assumed the gospel and emphasized the social and political commitments. The present generation identifies itself

---

1. Robert Farrar Capon, *Between Noon and Three: Romance, Law, and the Outrage of Grace* (Grand Rapids: Eerdmans, 1997), pp.109-10.

with the social and political commitments, while the gospel is variously confessed or disowned; it no longer lies at the heart of the belief system of some who call themselves Mennonites.[2]

The gospel was first cherished, then assumed, then lost. Such a process of spiritual devolution is not, of course, limited to a particular branch of the church. Left in neutral, all of us tend to slide away from the wonder of the gospel. My aim in this book is to help us cherish the gospel.

Easier said than done. However much we may pay tribute to grace with our lips, our hearts are so thoroughly marinated in law that the Christian life must be, at core, one of continually bathing our hearts and minds in gospel grace. We are addicted to law. Conforming our lives to a moral framework, playing by the rules, meeting a minimum standard — this feels normal. And it is how we naturally seek to cure that deep sense of inadequacy within. The real question is not how to avoid becoming a Pharisee; the question is how to recover from being the Pharisees that we all — right from the womb — already are.

Law feels safe; grace feels risky. Rule-keeping breeds a sense of manageability; grace feels like moral vertigo. After all, if all that we are is by grace, then there is no limit to what God can ask of us. But if some corner of our virtue is due to personal contribution, there is a ceiling on what God can ask of us. He can bring us only so far. He can ask only so much.

2. D. A. Carson, *The Cross and Christian Ministry: Leadership Lessons From 1 Corinthians* (Grand Rapids: Baker, 1993), p.63.

Such is not the call of Christ. The Jesus of the Gospels defies our domesticated, play-by-the-rules morality. It was the most extravagant sinners of Jesus' day who received his most compassionate welcome; it was the most scrupulously law-abiding people who were the objects of his most searing denunciation. The point is not that we should therefore take up sin. It is that we should lay down the silly insistence on leveraging our sense of self-worth with an ongoing moral record. Better a life of sin with penitence than a life of obedience without it.

This book is a call to embrace the flooding liberations of the gospel *all the way down* — not the decaffeinated grace that pats us on the hand, ignores our deepest rebellions, and doesn't change us, but the high-octane grace that takes our conscience by the scruff of the neck and breathes new life into us with a pardon so scandalous that we cannot help but be changed. This book is a brotherly exhortation to blow aside the hazy cloud of condemnation that hangs over us throughout the day with the strong wind of gospel grace.

You 'are not under law but under grace' (Rom. 6:14). Jesus is real; grace is subversive; life is short; risk is good. For many of us the time has come to abandon once and for all our play-it-safe, toe-dabbling Christianity and dive in. It's time, as Capon put it, to get drunk on grace — two-hundred-proof, subversive grace. Jesus doesn't crowbar us into change. He surprises us into change.

This book exists to stoke the fires of grace renewal already spreading throughout the twenty-first-century church.

Something of a resurgence of the gospel has been taking place today across various swathes of the Christian church. We must, of course, avoid facile generalizations. Yet it is evident from today's preaching and teaching, books and blogs, conferences and coalitions, that the gospel of grace is being wonderfully reasserted and cherished. Many have been walking with the Lord for years, yet are only now discovering the new mental and emotional universe of *grace*.

All this we happily receive from the hand of the Lord. The need of the hour, however, is neither self-congratulation nor smug diagnosis of who 'gets' the gospel of grace. The need of the hour is deeper reverence, new levels of wonder at the kindness shown to us, and a whispered prayer that the good news of God's free mercy in Christ would spread with a continued contagion with effects that will be felt for generations to come.

The spreading of that contagion is the reason for this book. *Surprised by Jesus* is divided into four parts, one on each Gospel's depiction of Jesus. Within each Gospel's treatment is a handful of short chapters. In Matthew, we see the surprise of disobedient obedience. Jesus' *definition of morality* is counterintuitive, contrary to all our expectations. Mark shows us the surprise of the king as a criminal. Jesus' *mission* is counterintuitive. In Luke, we are confronted with the surprise of outsiders becoming the insiders, and insiders, oddly, becoming the outsiders. Jesus' *community* is counterintuitive. And in John, we see the surprise of the Creator taking on flesh and blood as a creature. Jesus' *identity* is counterintuitive.

In theological terms, our treatment of Matthew lies in the realm of morality, of Mark in atonement, of Luke in ecclesiology (the doctrine of the church), and of John in Christology. Time and again, our intuitive expectations of who Jesus is and what he has come to do are turned upside down — whom he excludes, what he came to do, whom he welcomes, and who he is. Such emphases are not mutually exclusive, of course. All four Gospel accounts teach us about all four of these theological areas. Still, for all their overlap, God has given us four accounts, not one. And in a way unique to each Gospel account, we see the perplexing compassion of Jesus confront our intuitive expectations about morality, atonement, ecclesiology, and Christology. The Jesus of the Gospels defies our safe, law-saturated, score-keeping existence.

Jesus is many things. But *predictable* is not on the list. He is not, in the words of Mr Beaver, 'safe'.[3] Startling, arresting, surprising, infuriating, perplexing, yes; but not bland and predictable. No sooner have we convinced ourselves that God is real and the Bible meaningful than Jesus, the real Jesus, arrives on the scene and turns all our intuitive expectations on their heads.

But though Jesus' intuition-defying grace surprises us, our confusion does not surprise him. He knows all about it. And he is a patient teacher, more patient and tender than we have yet dared to believe.

So be surprised, with me, by the real Jesus.

---

3. C. S. Lewis, *The Lion, the Witch, and the Wardrobe* (New York: HarperCollins, 1978), p.86.

Part 1 – Matthew:
The surprise of
disobedient obedience

1.

JESUS' DEFINITION
OF MORALITY

OBEDIENCE CAN BE DAMNING.

Paul Tournier, the French psychologist of the last century, helps us to see why. 'The strange paradox present on every page of the Gospels,' he writes of Jesus' ministry, 'and which we can verify any day, is that it is not guilt which is the obstacle to grace, as moralism supposes. On the contrary, it is the repression of guilt, self-justification, genuine self-righteousness and smugness which is the obstacle.' Consequently, 'Before Jesus there are not two opposed human categories, the guilty and the righteous; there are only the guilty.'[4]

The deepest distinction among human beings is not between the bad and the good, but between those who *know* they are bad and those who do not. Yet, strangely, it is not the blatantly

---

4. Paul Tournier, *Guilt and Grace: A Psychological Study*, trans. Arthur W. Heathcote (New York: Harper & Row, 1962), pp.136, 112.

wicked who have the greatest difficulty seeing this, but the carefully obedient. Jesus consistently exposes the guilt, writes Tournier, of 'the moral and scrupulous people, by proclaiming that all men are equally sinful despite all their efforts, so that not by showing off their vaunted impeccability, but by confessing their guilt, by repentance, will they find the grace which erases it'.[5] Scrupulous 'obedience' is, more often than we are aware, thinly veiled *disobedience*. Obedience, therefore, can be damning.

Nowhere is this put more sharply than in Matthew's Gospel. To see it we will look at Jesus' teaching on life in the kingdom of God in Matthew 19 – 20. Here we find most clearly the great surprise of Matthew: that the strange key to participation in the joys of God's kingdom is not qualifying ourselves for it, but frankly acknowledging our disqualification — a disqualification that manifests itself not only in rule-breaking, but also in rule-keeping. Keeping the rules no more extinguishes the sin in our hearts than buckets of gasoline extinguish the flames in our fireplace. Matthew helps us to see this.

First we will focus on a portion of his Gospel, making some brief observations along the way. After plowing up the soil we will do some harvesting, tying it all together and seeing a common thread running throughout this section of Matthew's account.

What's the least I can do?

Matthew 18 – 20 portrays what life in the kingdom of God is meant to look like. And time after time a common question pops up, despite being asked by very different kinds of people.

---

5. *Ibid.*, p.122.

That question is: 'What's the least I can do?'

In Matthew 18:21-35 Peter asks Jesus how often he is required to forgive his brother. 'As many as seven times?' (18:21). 'Where is the bar set, Jesus? At what point can I finally be free to stop having to forgive?' Peter is asking what the least is that he can do with respect to forgiveness.

The very next account is a conversation between Jesus and the Pharisees (19:1-12). Yet the same issue of the heart lies underneath the external distinctions between the blue-collar fishermen who had given up everything to follow Jesus and the morally meticulous Pharisees who felt threatened by Jesus. For, as the Pharisees ask Jesus about divorce, essentially they enquire of him, 'What's the least I can do with respect to marriage?' (see 19:3). 'At what point have I fulfilled what the Jewish law requires of me in the marital realm?'

Finally, after Jesus rebukes his disciples for prohibiting the little children from coming to him (19:13-15 — a passage to which we will return), a rich young man approaches Jesus wondering what he must do to have eternal life (19:16-22). His query climaxes these three accounts by presenting us with the question that is behind the other questions. He asks, 'What's the least I can do with respect to obedience?'

In all three cases we are dealing with the same question in different clothing, yet this third instance takes us to the root of all three. Here we have come to the common concern raised by Peter, the Pharisees, and the rich young man. 'What is the minimum obedience I can render,' each asks, 'to get God off my back?'

Let's pick up the story at the young man's question and listen to Jesus, allowing this third and final conversation to launch us into the rest of Matthew 19 – 20.

Morality management

'Teacher, what good deed must I do to have eternal life?' (19:16). Here is a man who has been able to pay for everything in life with money — can't he also pay his way into eternal life with obedience?

Yet it's hard to get the right answer when you ask the wrong question. For right from the start we notice that this young man has not yet learned what Tournier has reminded us of: the question is not, 'Who will make the cut and be righteous?' but 'Who will admit that he can never make the cut?' A high-school freshman doesn't ask what blood type he is required to have in order to qualify for the football team; there is no right answer because the very question betrays a misunderstanding of what it takes in order to be on the team. Blood type is important, but irrelevant to gaining access to the football team. Obedience is important, but irrelevant to gaining access to eternal life. Heaven is not won with obedience. It is given.

Still, Jesus plays along:

> And he said to him, 'Why do you ask me about what is good? There is only one who is good. If you would enter life, keep the commandments.' He said to him, 'Which ones?' And Jesus said, 'You shall not murder,

You shall not commit adultery, You shall not steal, You shall not bear false witness, Honor your father and mother, and, You shall love your neighbor as yourself' (19:17-19).

From the perspective of the Bible there are two ways to sum up the Old Testament law. One is the Ten Commandments (Exod. 20:3-17; Deut. 5:7-22). The other is the double command to 'love the LORD your God with all your heart and with all your soul and with all your might' (Deut. 6:5) and to 'love your neighbor as yourself' (Lev. 19:18), which is how Jesus himself sums up the law in Matthew 22:37-40. In both lists, we have vertical elements followed by horizontal elements. Both lists start with our relationship with God and then move into our relationships with others. Here in Matthew 19, Jesus extracts the horizontal dimension to both summaries of the law and puts them before the young man. Of the Ten Commandments Jesus has ignored numbers one through four, and of the double commandment he has ignored the first part. In both cases, the vertical dimension is omitted.

Is this, however, completely accurate? Upon closer scrutiny, we see that this is not quite true. Jesus has quoted only five of the six horizontal commandments from the Decalogue. One is left out — the Tenth Commandment, which prohibits coveting. Why would Jesus leave this one off the list?

Jesus has bypassed this final horizontal commandment for the same reason that it is the sole commandment mentioned by Paul in Romans 7 as having aroused sin within him: it is the one horizontal commandment that addresses the heart.[6] Murder, adultery, theft, and the others, are all observable sins. Coveting is a sin of the heart. It is internal, invisible.

Jesus has put before the rich young man all the commandments that are, at first glance, externally manageable.

Exposing our idols

Consequently, the young man replies with confidence: 'All these I have kept.' He checks off each in turn. Yet the question remains: 'What do I still lack?' Even upon such brazen moral optimism, the young man knows something is not right. Those of us who believe ourselves to have kept the rules before God know the surprising emptiness resulting from such rigorous, though hollow, obedience. Swiss theologian Adolf Schlatter aptly called this young man's morality 'dry foliage'.[7]

> Jesus said to him, 'If you would be perfect, go, sell what you possess and give to the poor, and you will have treasure in heaven; and come, follow me.' When the young man heard this he went away sorrowful, for he had great possessions (19:21-22).

---

6. This is well articulated by Question 113 of the *Heidelberg Catechism*: '*Question*: What is God's will for you in the tenth commandment? *Answer*: That not even the slightest thought or desire contrary to any of God's commandments should ever arise in my heart. Rather, with all my heart I should always hate sin and take pleasure in whatever is right.'
7. Adolf Schlatter, 'Moral oder Evangelium?' ('Morality or Gospel?'), in *Gesunde Lehre: Reden und Aufsätze* (Velbert: Freizeiten Verlag, 1929), p.94.

With Jesus' climactic exhortation to renounce all in order to follow him, he was not dangling the carrot of law-keeping in front of this young man, egging him on in his self-justifying law-observance. Instead Jesus has lovingly set up the young man to show him his idolatry. Jesus has slipped in the First Commandment ('You shall have no other gods before me', Exod. 20:3) without the young man noticing. He exposes the man's sin not by showing him that he needed to give away his material possessions to follow God, but that his material possessions *were* his god. And as Martin Luther has pointed out, there is no breaking of commandments numbers two to ten without first breaking commandment number one.[8] If we

8. Martin Luther, *A Treatise on Good Works*, in *Luther's Works*, vol. 44: *The Christian in Society I*, ed. James Atkinson (Philadelphia: Fortress, 1966), pp.30-31; *Luther's Works*, vol. 51: *Sermons I*, ed. John W. Doberstein (Philadelphia: Fortress, 1959), pp.144, 161. See also Robert Kolb and Charles P. Arand, *The Genius of Luther's Theology: A Wittenberg Way of Thinking for the Contemporary Church* (Grand Rapids: Baker, 2008), pp.68, 153.

G. C. Berkouwer makes the same observation about the nature of the First Commandment, though in a less developed way, in *Faith and Sanctification*, trans. John Vriend (Grand Rapids: Eerdmans, 1952), pp.184-85.

Luther further helps us to see that the First Commandment is an implicit call to justification by faith. Because idolatry is justification by an idol (i.e. materialism is justification by financial security; sexual immorality is justification by pleasure; self-promotion is justification by the approval of others), the First Commandment is in fact a call to God's people not to have any lesser forms of justification before God. 'You shall have no other gods before me' means, if nothing else, 'You shall trust me; you shall seek your sense of self-worth — that is, your justification — in nothing less than me, the only one who can provide it and the only one in whom it is worthy to be sought' (see *Luther's Works*, vol. 44, pp.33-34; vol. 51, p.17).

dishonor our parents, we have broken commandments one and five; our god is independence. If we commit adultery, we have broken commandments one and seven; our god is sex. And if we love money, we have broken commandments one and ten; our god is material possessions. The First Commandment is the filter through which every sin passes.

In view of how seriously this young man took his morality, it is safe to assume that he made the appropriate Jewish tithes. But Jesus calls him to give away all that he owned because mere tithing allows a materialist to keep his idol basically intact. Jesus goes straight to the core of the young man's deepest affection: his financial security. His heart is exposed. And, sadly, like a child suffering from an irritating rash who prefers scratching to a healing steroid, the young man prefers the idol — and goes away sorrowful.

Elephants and sub-atomic particles

At this point Jesus seizes the opportunity to teach his disciples a lesson:

> And Jesus said to his disciples, 'Truly, I say to you, only with difficulty will a rich person enter the kingdom of heaven. Again I tell you, it is easier for a camel to go through the eye of a needle than for a rich person to enter the kingdom of God.' When the disciples heard this, they were greatly astonished, saying, 'Who then can be saved?' (19:23-25).

Jesus' metaphor of a camel and a needle is not meant to say anything particularly cryptic. He simply calls to mind the largest known animal and the smallest known opening of the time. Had he been speaking today, he might have said it is easier for an elephant to pass through a sub-atomic particle than for a rich man to enter the kingdom of God. The point is the same either way. It's impossible.

Why are the disciples so troubled, though? It's puzzling at first to modern readers why they should be so flabbergasted. If it's hard for the rich to enter the kingdom of God, then isn't the solution simply to avoid wealth? Why don't the disciples simply resolve to live in either the lower or middle class of society? The reason is that this was not how life worked for the first-century Jew. Financial gain was seen as a direct sign of God's approval. It was axiomatic that 'The blessing of the LORD makes rich' (Prov. 10:22). Material blessing was viewed as linked to spiritual blessing (Deut. 28:1-6, 8, 11-12). When the disciples ask, 'Who then can be saved?' they are saying, 'If those at the top of the social stratosphere, upon whom God has so clearly smiled, can't get in, what hope is there for the rest of us, who don't have that kind of obvious divine favor?'[9]

---

9. The matter is a bit more complex than this — some proverbs speak of the blessing of wealth (Prov. 8:18; 10:4, 15, 22; 14:24; 22:4), others of the dangers of wealth (Prov. 11:4, 28; cf. Prov. 23:4; 28:22). For a balanced assessment of the multifaceted biblical teaching on wealth, see Craig L. Blomberg, *Neither Poverty nor Riches: A Biblical Theology of Possessions* (NSBT 7; Downers Grove, Ill.: InterVarsity, 1999). The point should stand, however, that first-century Jews would view wealth as a divine blessing far more readily than twenty-first century Western believers; see, for example, Ben Witherington III, *Jesus the Sage: The Pilgrimage of Wisdom* (Minneapolis: Augsburg Fortress,

Jesus responds enigmatically, affirming their dismay before rebuilding hope on the proper foundation: 'But Jesus looked at them and said, "With man this is impossible, but with God all things are possible"' (19:26). 'It's worse than you think,' says Jesus — 'and so much better.' According to your intuitive, natural, moralizing, domesticated, get-what-you-work-for understanding of the way you think God relates to people, yes, this is impossible. But with God — according to the wild, lavish, all out of proportion, get-far-more-than-you-asked-for-as-long-as-you-don't-try-to-pay-for-it understanding of the way God relates to his people, all things are possible. 'Above the impossibilities of our own making,' wrote Schlatter, 'stands the omnipotence of grace.'[10]

Heirs don't earn

'Then Peter said in reply, "See, we have left everything and followed you. What then will we have?"' (19:27). As with the rich young man's misguided question in verse 16, so here with Peter's — it's the wrong question. Jesus nevertheless responds by assuring Peter and the disciples that all they have done will be abundantly rewarded in the new earth: 'everyone who has left houses or brothers or sisters or father or mother or children or lands, for my name's sake, will receive a hundredfold and will inherit eternal life' (19:29).

1994), p.166; Robert H. Gundry, *A Survey of the New Testament* (Grand Rapids: Zondervan, 4th edition, 2003), p.146. On the divine blessing of wealth see also 1 Kings 3:10-13; Job 42:12; Eccles. 5:19.

10. Adolf Schlatter, *Do We Know Jesus? Daily Insights for the Mind and Soul*, trans. Andreas J. Köstenberger and Robert W. Yarbrough (Grand Rapids: Kregel, 2005), p.193.

Two observations help us make sense of what's happening here. First, this is not the only reference to 'eternal life' we have seen in Matthew 19. Back in verse 16, the rich young man asked what he had to do to get it. But notice that the young man spoke about *earning* eternal life. Verse 16 literally reads, 'What must I do in order that I might have eternal life?' In verse 29, however, Jesus speaks of those who renounce all for his sake as *inheriting* eternal life. Heirs don't earn. They receive, simply by being born into the family, by no virtue of their own. A billionaire's only son doesn't have to *do* anything to inherit a fortune when his father passes away.

Secondly, Peter clearly viewed himself as the polar opposite of the rich young man. As the young man slowly disappears around a bend in the road, Peter turns to Jesus and reminds him, 'We have left everything...' While the young man refused to leave house and home to follow Jesus, Peter had done precisely that (see also 4:18-20). Yet although the young man and Peter responded to Jesus in opposite ways, *they were treating discipleship in precisely the same way*. Both viewed loyalty to Jesus as a financial transaction. The young man wanted his money, so he didn't follow Jesus. Peter wanted a reward, so he did. Neither wanted Jesus. Is there really much of a difference whether disobedience or obedience was the substitute savior? As Lewis once wrote, 'Does it matter to a man dying in a desert by which choice of route he missed the only well?'[11]

---

11. C. S. Lewis, 'A Slip of the Tongue,' in *The Weight of Glory and Other Addresses* (New York: Touchstone, 1996), p.142.

Overturning not only the rich young man's refusal to sacrifice all, but also Peter's commitment to sacrifice all, Jesus immediately follows up his assurance of reward to his loyal followers with the strange comment: 'But many who are first will be last, and the last first' (19:30).

Now what in the world does that mean?

The last will be first

Evidently the disciples were wondering the same thing. For, as he so often did, Jesus told a story. He spoke of a landowner who hired workers for his vineyard at different points throughout the day and yet paid each a full day's wage.

In order to show just how upside-down Jesus' story would have sounded to a first-century Jew, listen to the words of a rabbi roughly around the time of Jesus in a commentary on part of the Old Testament law. This rabbi is reflecting on Leviticus 26, which speaks of a series of blessings for obedience. At one point God describes the way he will respond to his people's obedience by assuring them, 'I will turn to you', which can also be translated, 'I will have regard for you' (Lev. 26:9). The mindset of this rabbi — my own default mindset, too — illuminates the dynamic of the heart Jesus is overturning.

'And I will have regard for you.' They told a parable. What is the matter like? It is like a king who hired many workers. There was one particular worker who had labored for him many days. The workers came to receive their payment and this worker entered with them. The king said to that worker, 'My son, I shall have special regard for you. These many who labored with me a little I shall pay a little. But I am about to settle a large account with you.' ... Therefore it is said, 'And I will have regard for you.'[12]

This is not evidence that the Jews were more self-righteous than other ancient people groups. Yet that is not because the Jews did *not* have a problem with self-righteousness, but because everyone else *does*. Judaism is no more 'legalistic' than any other religion so long as that religion is made up of humans, for the propensity to earn rather than receive God's

---

12. *Sifra Behuqqotai pereq* 2:5, quoted in E. P. Sanders, *Paul and Palestinian Judaism: A Comparison of Patterns of Religion* (Minneapolis: Fortress, 1977), p.118. A similar account was told 300 years after Jesus by a rabbi in a funeral oration for a young man who had died at the age of twenty-eight. According to Joachim Jeremias' modern rendering of the parable, the rabbi 'began by saying that the situation was like that of a king who had hired a great number of laborers. Two hours after the work had begun, he inspected them, and saw that one of them was more skillful and industrious than the others... When the laborers came to receive their wages, this one received the same amount as the others. Then they grumbled and said, "We have worked the whole day, against this man's two hours, and yet you have paid him the full day's wages." The king replied, "I have not wronged you; this laborer has done more in two hours than you have done in the whole day"' (Joachim Jeremias, *Rediscovering the Parables*, New York: Scribner's, 1966, p.110). Jeremias points out that, among many striking similarities between this parable and that of Jesus, the worker in the Jewish parable, despite working such a short amount of time, produced more than the others; in Jesus' parable, the later hired workers can plead nothing but the kindness of the one who hired them.

favor is a human, not a Jewish, problem.[13]

Now let's listen to how *Jesus* explains God's response to our hard work on his behalf.

For the kingdom of heaven is like a master of a house who went out early in the morning to hire laborers for his vineyard. After agreeing with the laborers for a denarius a day, he sent them into his vineyard. And going out about the third hour he saw others standing idle in the marketplace, and to them he said, 'You go into the vineyard too, and whatever is right I will give you.' So they went. Going out again about the sixth hour and the ninth hour, he did the same. And about the eleventh hour he went out and found others standing. And he said to them, 'Why do you stand here idle all day?' They said to him, 'Because no one has hired us.' He said to them, 'You go into the vineyard too.' And when evening came, the owner of the vineyard said to his foreman, 'Call the laborers and pay them their wages, beginning with the last, up to the first.' And when those hired about the eleventh hour came, each of them received a denarius. Now when those hired

13. See Helmut Thielicke, *The Waiting Father: Sermons on the Parables of Jesus*, trans. John W. Doberstein (New York: Harper & Row, 1959), p.117; Peter Stuhlmacher, *Revisiting Paul's Doctrine of Justification: A Challenge to the New Perspective*, trans. Daniel P. Bailey (Downers Grove, Ill.: InterVarsity, 2001), pp.86-87; Thomas R. Schreiner, *Paul, Apostle of God's Glory in Christ: A Pauline Theology* (Downers Grove, Ill.: InterVarsity, 2006), p.121.

first came, they thought they would receive more, but each of them also received a denarius. And on receiving it they grumbled at the master of the house, saying, 'These last worked only one hour, and you have made them equal to us who have borne the burden of the day and the scorching heat.' But he replied to one of them, 'Friend, I am doing you no wrong. Did you not agree with me for a denarius? Take what belongs to you and go. I choose to give to this last worker as I give to you. Am I not allowed to do what I choose with what belongs to me? Or do you begrudge my generosity?' So the last will be first, and the first last' (20:1-16).

Not what we earn but what we need
With the last sentence of the parable, Jesus returns to his words in the last verse of Matthew 19: the first will be last and the last first. This is his way of indicating that the parable is fleshing out what he meant at the end of chapter 19 when he first stated this principle.

What, then, is this parable communicating?

The point is twofold: first, with respect to those hired later in the day; and, secondly, with respect to those hired earlier. The second group, the workers who were hired early, will be our main focus.

We see the compassionate generosity of the landowner who treats the workers hired later in the day not according to what they deserve, but according to what they *need*. A denarius was a day's wage. It would feed the employee's family for that day (see Deut. 24:14-15). Yet the workers did not even seek out the job. The landowner sought the workers. Indeed, the landowner did not even leave it to his foreman to seek out employees; the landowner sought them out himself. Drawing on sixty years' experience living and teaching the New Testament in Egypt, Lebanon, Jerusalem, and Cyprus, Professor Kenneth Bailey helps us understand the strangeness of the landowner's actions here:

> Landowners in the Middle East are known traditionally to be gentlemen farmers. They hire others to work the land and appoint a foreman/steward to manage the estate. A traditional landowner may give his steward careful instructions in the morning and ask for a report at the end of the day. But to make the trek, in person, from the farm to the market and back five times in a single day is unheard of. That is the manager's job.[14]

And, besides, how much help, we might ask, could really have been provided in the vineyard by that final wave of recruitment? These tardiest of workers were hired at the eleventh hour, or 5 p.m. In a workday that went from sunrise (6 a.m.) to sunset (6 p.m.), this meant the landowner got one hour of work out of them. In fact we read, not that the workers started work at the eleventh hour, but that the landowner 'went out' looking for more workers at the eleventh hour (20:6). By the time they

---

14. Kenneth E. Bailey, *Jesus through Middle Eastern Eyes: Cultural Studies in the Gospels* (Downers Grove, Ill.: InterVarsity, 2008), p.363.

all returned to the vineyard and the foreman explained the job to them, perhaps it was only thirty minutes or less of actual work that the landowner got out of these latecomers.

The landowner did not need the workers; the workers needed the landowner. As Jerry Bridges points out, the parable shows us that God doesn't give us what we've earned. He gives us what we need.[15]

When our gratitude for grace received devolves into Jonah-like resentment that others less deserving have received grace, we show that we have not, in fact, understood the grace we ourselves received. For if grace is truly grace, freely granted, and not tethered to any personal merit or demerit, then it is impossible for anyone to deserve it any less or any more than the next person. Bailey rightly points out that the grouchy workers are not grouchy because they are underpaid but because others, in their perception, are overpaid:

> The story focuses on an equation filled with amazing grace, which is resented by those who feel that they have earned their way to more… The complaint is from the justly paid who cannot tolerate grace… Grace is not only amazing, it is also — for certain types — *infuriating!*[16]

Jesus surprises us with his surprising grace.

---

15. Jerry Bridges, *Transforming Grace: Living Confidently in God's Unfailing Love* (Colorado Spring, Col.: NavPress, 1991), pp.48-51, 613.
16. Bailey, *Jesus through Middle Eastern Eyes*, pp.360-61.

2.

THE PHARISEE WITHIN

NOW WE MOVE from plowing up the soil of Matthew 19 – 20 to harvesting what we have seen and funneling it into our own lives. The workers who were hired earlier in the day showed us that the greatest obstacle to glad, fruitful life in the kingdom of God is disobedient obedience.

Reluctant taxpayers

The reason we looked at such a large portion of Matthew is that the mindset of the early hired workers illustrates exactly the mindset of both the rich young man and Peter. A common problem infected them all. They were operating out of the intuitive assumption that life in the kingdom was about receiving *in addition to* earning, rather than receiving *to the exclusion of* earning. They thought the only alternative to being bad was being good, failing to see that being good can be just as empty of the gospel as being bad. They thought there was one way to reject God, when in fact there are two:

hard-hearted disobedience and hard-hearted obedience. The only difference is that the first kind *knows* it is rejecting God. The gospel is God's provision of free acceptance in Christ utterly apart from our own detraction from, or contribution to, that acceptance. If that is so, then not only moral failing but also moral success is excluded from God's love for us.

Yet the rich young man, Peter, and the early hired workers were all treating their relationship with God like a savings account — put in a little obedience each day, keep track as you go ('all these I have kept'; 'we have left everything'), tally it up, and hope that we will have enough to live on at the end. Such a mindset backfires because it denies both the inadequacy of our own moral resources (as a result of our sin) and the adequacy of God's divine provision (on account of Christ's work). Put differently, such obedience is actually disobedience because it treats obedience like paying a tax. The metaphor belongs to C. S. Lewis:

> Our temptation is to look eagerly for the minimum that will be accepted [i.e., what's the least I can do?]. We are in fact very like honest but reluctant taxpayers. We approve of an income tax in principle. We make our returns truthfully. But we dread a rise in the tax. We are very careful to pay no more than is necessary. And we hope — we very ardently hope — that after we have paid it there will still be enough left to live on.[17]

---

17. Lewis, 'Slip of the Tongue,' p.140. Similarly, Schlatter, *Do We Know Jesus?*, pp.135-36.

Obedience rendered to God with the same attitude with which we pay our taxes is not obedience at all. It is disobedience. It is what Schlatter rightly described as 'the monster of an impious piety'.[18]

To qualify or not to qualify?

The danger of obedience can be further illuminated by framing it in terms of *qualification*. For the string of passages which runs from the account of the little children being discouraged from coming to Jesus (19:13-15) through to the end of the parable (20:16) is all connected by a single thread, the main point Matthew wants us to see about how life in the kingdom works. That point is that, in the kingdom of God, the one thing that qualifies you is knowing that you don't qualify, and the one thing that disqualifies you is thinking that you do.

Consider the string of accounts in Matthew's Gospel that we have touched upon. In every passage, a central character assumes that one has to 'qualify' to gain some corresponding approval.

- The disciples thought that little children needed to qualify by being a certain age in order to gain Jesus' attention (19:13-15).

- The rich young man thought he needed to qualify by law-keeping in order to gain eternal life (19:16-22).

18. Adolf Schlatter, *The History of the Christ*, trans. Andreas J. Köstenberger (Grand Rapids: Baker, 1997), p.152; cf. pp.217-29, 328-29.

- Peter and company thought they had to qualify by making a sacrifice in order to gain a reward (19:23-30).

- The workers who were hired early thought that all employees had to qualify by doing sufficient work in order to gain a day's wage (20:1-16).

In our moments of spiritual sanity, you and I know that we are no different. We tend to assume that in order for God to approve of us — *really* approve of us — we need to qualify. And at that moment, the gospel has shifted out of the burning fireplace of our heart and into the cold and dusty attic of self-contribution.

A Christian is not someone who has been enrolled in the moral hall of fame. A Christian is a happily recovering Pharisee.

Evil rule-keeping

I say 'Pharisee' because this disobedient obedience is present all through Matthew's Gospel and is clearest in the Pharisees' antagonistic confrontations with Jesus — confrontations that make about as much sense as a diabetes patient angrily confronting the medic who has arrived with a life-saving dose of insulin. If anyone ought to have rejoiced at Christ's coming it was the scribes and Pharisees. They were the erudite seminary professors of the day. They were the ones who knew the Scriptures that contained God's ancient promises and the whispered prophecies of a coming Savior.

To be sure, some of them did recognize in Jesus the hope of Israel and the Savior of the world (Mark 12:28-34; John 3:12;

THE PHARISEE WITHIN

7:50-52; 19:39). Yet time and again these religious leaders, on the whole, rejected Jesus and his teaching. How so? Not because they threw out all the rules. On the contrary, in terms of the law, they were grade-A students. They kept all the rules. They were obedient. But it was a disobedient obedience. It was, as Augustine put it, vice clothed in virtue.[19] It was self-serving obedience, comparing themselves with others. The Pharisees were not less evil than the immoral. While the immoral were evil and were upfront about it, the Pharisees were evil on the inside but masked it, adding hypocrisy to their already culpable hearts.[20] In Matthew 12, Jesus called them a 'brood of vipers' and articulated the discrepancy between what they said on the outside and what was true of them on the inside: 'How can you speak good, when you are evil?' (12:34). Yes, we can be evil by throwing out all the rules. But we can be just as evil by keeping all the rules.

The scribes and Pharisees epitomized such disobedient obedience, earning them searing denunciations from Jesus in places such as Matthew 23, where he pronounces seven woes on them. Certainly we do not want to lump all the Pharisees together in this unflattering appraisal. Yet, according to Matthew, these men were the single greatest hindrance to Jesus' public ministry. Their hatred of him ran so deep that they repeatedly plotted how to kill him (12:14; 21:46; 22:15).

19. Augustine, *City of God*, ed. Vernon J. Bourke; trans. Gerald G. Walsh *et al.* (Garden City, N.Y.: Image, 1958), xix.25; cf. v.20.
20. On the internal nature of authentic discipleship, see Francis Schaeffer, *True Spirituality* (Wheaton, Ill.: Tyndale House, 1971), pp.114, 116, 120-21.

The point of bringing in the Pharisees is partly to show that disobedient obedience is a problem throughout Matthew, yet also to see that in Matthew 19 – 20 we discover that there is something of a Pharisee even in Jesus' most devoted followers. The greatest danger for followers of Christ is not the ways they fail him, but the ways they succeed. Failures, as we will see further in our discussion of Luke, are precisely the kind of people God is looking for. For failures instinctively understand how to open the windows of their heart to let in help. Those who think they have made a success of their lives invariably turn in on themselves in satisfied self-reliance. Penitent hookers enter heaven ahead of smug virgins (21:31).

This is why Jonathan Edwards wrote his famous treatise on *Religious Affections*. In the wake of a local revival (1734–35) and then the trans-Atlantic revival known today as the Great Awakening (1740–42), Edwards increasingly saw the need to distinguish between those who had been authentically affected by God's Spirit and those who *seemed* to display authentic spiritual experience yet who had not been truly touched by God. *Religious Affections* is a sustained reflection on this challenging kind of discernment. What is remarkable is that in this treatise Edwards is not comparing disobedient and obedient people. He is looking at two different kinds of uprightness. Both zealously sing God's praises, tell others of their salvation, and quote the Bible — yet for some it is rooted in self-love, not love for Christ. Edwards is not distinguishing between immoral and moral people, but between artificially moral and authentically moral people.[21]

A theme throughout Matthew

The startling contrast is found throughout Matthew, such as in the Sermon on the Mount in Matthew 5 – 7. Against what we expect, Jesus does not contrast those who clearly reject God's will with those who submit themselves to God's will. Rather, he contrasts those who obey God for the sake of being seen by others with those who obey God for the sake of love for him.[22] Jesus warns his disciples not of the danger of failing to practice righteousness, but the danger of practicing righteousness before others. The paradoxical dimension of the Sermon on the Mount is sharply put by Adolf Schlatter in his overview of New Testament theology. In a section strikingly entitled 'The Repentance of the Pious', Schlatter reminds us of the surprising nature of the audience to whom Jesus was speaking:

---

21. Geerhardus Vos draws the same contrast in his 1903 article, 'The Alleged Legalism in Paul's Doctrine of Justification,' in *Redemptive History and Biblical Interpretation*, ed. Richard Gaffin (Phillipsburg, N.J.: P&R, 1980), p.396. See also Gerhard O. Forde, *Justification by Faith: A Matter of Death and Life* (Philadelphia: Fortress, 1982), pp.22-35, 51, 53, 85-86; Gerhard O. Forde, *On Being a Theologian of the Cross: Reflections on Luther's Heidelberg Disputation, 1518* (Grand Rapids: Eerdmans, 1997), pp.26-27.
22. J. C. Ryle, *Ryle's Expository Thoughts on the Gospels: Matthew* (Grand Rapids: Zondervan, n.d.), p.47; Schlatter, *History of the Christ*, pp.149-52.

Jesus pitched the Sermon on the Mount against those who condemned murder and avoided adultery as sin, not against those who murdered and followed every lust ... against those who loved the friend, not against the selfish who loved merely themselves; against those who were ready benefactors and fasted and prayed, not against those who neglected to do so.[23]

Jesus was not preaching to the perilously immoral, but to the perilously moral. 'Jesus did not call the pious to repentance simply because he rejected their sin,' Schlatter later remarks, 'but also because he condemned their righteousness.'[24]

The upside-down problem of disobedient obedience is seen not only in the Sermon on the Mount, but also in Jesus' interactions with his professing followers (Matt. 18 – 20) and in his clashes with the religious leaders of the day (Matt. 12; 23).

The kind of disobedient obedience we have seen in Matthew is not, however, a first-century phenomenon. Not only the rich young man, Peter, and the early workers, but you and I, too, have a Pharisee inside us. It isn't going away by more trenchantly dutiful living — this is just the thing that feeds the Pharisee within. Raw obedience can no more root out our moralistic tendencies than pouring fertilizer on the weeds in our front yard roots out these botanical pests.

---

23. Schlatter, *History of the Christ*, pp.149-50.
24. *Ibid.*, p.150.

3.

HEART RESPONSE

HOW, THEN, DO we get gospel traction in our lives? What are we to do if, as one theologian puts it, 'religion and irreligion are equally helpless'?[25] How do we live gospel-fueled lives in the face of such overwhelming internal resistance? The same way that we get rid of the weeds: dig them out, roots and all — including what's underneath the surface.

Four reminders in particular will help us.

Obedience: a means or an end?

First, we must recognize obedience not as a means, but as an end. What I mean is this. The rich young man viewed his law-keeping as a means to the end of earning eternal life. Peter viewed his sacrifice as a means to the end of great reward. The all-day workers in Jesus' parable viewed their job as a means

25. Robert W. Jenson, *America's Theologian: A Recommendation of Jonathan Edwards* (Oxford: Oxford University Press, 1992), p.64; see also pp.82-83.

to the end of earning a wage. All assumed that obedience was the means to some other end, failing to see that obedience — true obedience, from the heart — is its own reward. To love God with all one's heart is not an avenue to some other end.[26]

To obey God 'from the heart' (Rom. 6:17) — that is, to love, adore, and enjoy him, feeding on him as a fire feeds on oxygen — is an end in itself. It is its own reward, because deeper obedience fosters deeper communing with God. Because God himself is the fuel on which we are made to run, such communion with him is the deepest and most solid joy we can know.

Gospel growth

Secondly, progressive growth in holiness is energized not by graduating on from the gospel of God's free grace, but by deeper reflection on the very gospel that captured us in the first place.[27]

26. Christian Smith discusses the prevalence of this 'instrumental' view of religion among young people in *Soul Searching: The Religious and Spiritual Lives of American Teenagers* (New York: Oxford University Press, 2005), pp.147-54.

27. See Berkouwer, *Faith and Sanctification*, pp.64, 77-78, 84, 93, 96, 193; also J. Gresham Machen, *What is Faith?* (London: Hodder & Stoughton, 1925), p.153; William E. Hulme, *Counseling and Theology* (Philadelphia: Fortress, 1956), pp.179-80, 184, 193-4; Jerry Bridges, *The Discipline of Grace: God's Role and Our Role in the Pursuit of Holiness* (Colorado Spring: NavPress, 1994), pp.29-93; Jerry Bridges, *The Gospel for Real Life* (Colorado Spring: NavPress, 2002), pp.173-83; C. J. Mahaney, *Living the Cross Centered Life* (Sisters, Ore.: Multnomah, 2006), pp.17-20, 147-56; Bryan Chapell, 'The Necessity of Preaching Grace for Progress in Sanctification,' in *All for Jesus: A Celebration of the 50th Anniversary of Covenant Theological Seminary*, ed. Sean Michael Lucas and Robert Peterson (Fearn, Scotland: Christian Focus, 2006), pp.47-60; Dennis E. Johnson, *Him We Proclaim: Preaching Christ from All the Scriptures* (Phillipsburg, N.J.: Presbyterian &

I wonder whether somewhere along the way you have been given an artificial picture of the Christian life. Maybe you have been taught (as I was) that the gospel is what bridges the gap between us and God, and that once this gap is bridged we 'move on' to discipleship — punctilious quiet times, regular witnessing, dutiful church involvement, faithful tithing. The gospel message that 'Christ died for our sins' (1 Cor. 15:3) initiates us into Christianity and then fades into the background in relevance. Or maybe you were taught that we should continue with the gospel but, somehow, its fire burns less brightly in your heart and mind than it once did.

The trouble is that moving on or moving away from the gospel is precisely the opposite of how the New Testament portrays the Christian life. The portrait of discipleship painted by the New Testament is that our first discovery of the gospel is the inauguration of an entire life of increasingly sensitized wonder at this grace. The gospel is not the runway to the Christian life — getting us off the ground at conversion and landing us in heaven at death, but irrelevant in between. The gospel is the engine — getting us off the ground, landing us, and keeping us in the air all along. In confronting Peter's racist favoritism, Paul wrote not that Peter needed to cultivate more effective discipleship strategies, but that his 'conduct was not in step with the

Reformed, 2007), pp.41-3, 55-57; Stephen Smallman, *The Walk: Steps for New and Renewed Followers of Jesus* (Phillipsburg, N.J.: Presbyterian & Reformed, 2009), pp.69-81, 215-16.

truth of the gospel' (Gal. 2:14). Was Peter a believer? Of course. But he needed to continue to grow in his reflection on the gospel itself, and live in accord with it. 'The truth of the gospel' was still sinking in.

Christian discipleship is not the process of getting in by grace and then becoming less and less dependent on that grace. It is, rather, becoming *more* dependent on grace. The engine of healthy sanctification (increase in holiness) is increasing awareness of justification (declaration of acquittal).[28] Our growth does not fuel our status; our status fuels our growth. When a caterpillar is given wings as it graduates on to become a butterfly, it does not then become less dependent on those wings. It grows ever more dependent upon them, learning to use them in increasing measure. Paul exhorted the Colossians to 'continue in the faith, stable and steadfast, not shifting from the hope of the gospel that you heard' (Col. 1:23; cf. Col. 2:5-6).

Though Peter was at times slow to understand this 'gospel growth' during Jesus' ministry (Matt. 19), and even about twenty years later (Gal. 2:14), he would come to truly grasp and be transformed by the gospel. Towards the end of his life, the ex-fisherman reminded his fellow believers that God's 'divine power has granted to us all things that pertain to life and godliness' (2 Peter 1:3). God

---

28. See Martyn Lloyd-Jones, *Spiritual Depression: Its Causes and Cure* (Grand Rapids: Eerdmans, 1965), p.25; Hulme, *Counseling and Theology*, p.180; Dane C. Ortlund, 'Sanctification by Justification: The Forgotten Insight of Bavinck and Berkouwer on Progressive Sanctification,' *Scottish Bulletin of Evangelical Theology* 28, 2010, pp.43-61.

supplies all we need — not just for getting in, but for life and godliness thereafter. A few verses later, after describing a list of the virtues of the healthy Christian, Peter gives an underlying principle for how such growth takes place: 'For whoever lacks these qualities is so short-sighted that he is blind, having forgotten that he was cleansed from his former sins' (2 Peter 1:9). Spiritual stagnancy results from *forgetting* the very gospel that brought us into the kingdom. Spiritual growth, cultivation of virtue, results from *remembering* the gospel. Forgiving grace is not an entrance ticket, to be torn up; it is the fresh air we now breathe, to be relished forever. 'The gospel is the food of faith,' wrote Dutch theologian Herman Bavinck, 'and must be known to be nourishment.'[29]

All this is not to deny the critical fruit that must be born in the life of a genuine believer, or the tremendous personal struggle that will be involved in sanctification (1 Cor. 15:10; Phil. 2:12-13; Col. 1:29). Christian growth is a process, and disciples of Jesus will either increasingly be conformed into the image of Christ (Rom. 8:29) or prove that they are not, after all, true disciples (3:8; 7:19, 22-23; John 15:1-2; James 3:11-12). The Christian life will often feel like two steps forward and three steps backward.

But the way sanctifying growth takes place is not, in essence, by redoubling moral efforts, writing out new

29. Herman Bavinck, *Reformed Dogmatics*, ed. John Bolt; trans. John Vriend (Grand Rapids: Baker, 4 vols., 2003–2008), vol. 4, p.96; see also vol. 3, p.528; vol. 4, pp.245, 248, 257.

resolutions, and intensifying spiritual disciplines. The fundamental means of change is deeper and deeper reflection on the very gospel that rescued us in the first place. It sounds backward, but the path to holiness is through (not beyond) the grace of the gospel, because only undeserved grace can truly melt and transform the heart. Disobedience is not healed with obedience. Morality can reform, but never transform, immorality. Immorality is transformed only by the free grace of God — grace so free that it will be misheard by some as a license to sin with impunity (see Rom. 5:20 – 6:1). The route by which the New Testament exhorts radical obedience is not by tempering grace, but by driving it home all the more deeply.

Morality: 'the greatest enemy'

What, then, is this gospel by which we are not only placed within God's family, but on which we reflect more deeply our whole lives long? This brings us to the third reminder. Here we return to a truth briefly touched upon in our observations on Jesus' parable in Matthew 20, where we unearthed the counterintuitive dimension to the gospel by stating that: in the kingdom of God, the one thing that *qualifies* us is knowing that we don't, and the one thing that *disqualifies* us is thinking that we do. In other words, all we need is to know our need. To put it briefly, the only thing to offer is the single statement: 'I have nothing to offer.'

Martin Luther, the sixteenth-century Reformer, wrote:

Grace is given freely to those without merits and the most undeserving, and is not obtained by any efforts, endeavors, or works, whether small or great, even of the best and most virtuous of men, though they seek and pursue righteousness with burning zeal.[30]

Not only does burning moral zeal *not* contribute to our standing before God, it can be positively blinding with regard to our true spiritual state. Edwards wrote that 'There is nothing that belongs to Christian experience that is more liable to a corrupt mixture than zeal.'[31] Perhaps this is why in more than one place in Matthew's Gospel Jesus called the most ethically assiduous leaders of his day 'blind guides' (15:14; 23:16, 24). Paul saw this in his fellow Jews, for he prayed for their salvation (Rom. 10:1) despite acknowledging their 'zeal for God' (Rom. 10:2).

Christianity is the unreligion. It turns all our religious instincts on their head. Jesus' parable is not an attempt to show us which religion is the right one; it is meant to show us that religion itself is not the answer. The apostle Paul

---

30. Martin Luther, *The Bondage of the Will*, in *Luther's Works*, ed. Philip S. Watson (Philadelphia: Fortress, 55 vols, 1972), vol. 33, p.318. Luther is commenting on Romans 9:30.

31. Jonathan Edwards, *Some Thoughts Concerning the Revival*, in *The Works of Jonathan Edwards*, ed. C. C. Goen (New Haven: Yale University Press, 1972), vol. 4, p.460. The subtle danger of religious zeal is a pervasive theme in Edwards; see, for example, *Distinguishing Marks of a Work of the Spirit of God*, in *Works of Jonathan Edwards*, vol. 4, pp.243, 287; *Some Thoughts Concerning the Revival*, pp.318-20, 429-30, 468.

looked back on a life of earnest religion and called it not only unhelpful but 'loss' (Phil. 3:7).[32]

The ancient Greeks told us to be moderate by knowing our inclinations. The Romans told us to be strong by ordering our lives. Buddhism tells us to be disillusioned by annihilating our consciousness. Hinduism tells us to be absorbed by merging our souls. Islam tells us to be submissive by subjecting our wills. Agnosticism tells us to be at peace by ignoring our doubts. Moralism tells us to be good by discharging our obligations. Only the gospel tells us to be free by acknowledging our failure.[33] Christianity is the unreligion because it is the one faith whose founder tells us to bring not our doing, but our need.

Our natural intuitions whisper to us that the way to avoid disobedience is obedience. Yet how easy it is to overlook the fact that it can be precisely our fraudulent obedience that keeps us from living, as Paul put it, 'in step with the truth of the gospel' (Gal. 2:14). We often hear in our churches of the danger of grace-resisting disobedience. Rarely do we hear of the danger of grace-forgetting obedience.

Martyn Lloyd-Jones, the British preacher of the twentieth century, rightly preached in 1959 that it is not immorality

---

32. Robert Jenson writes, 'It is a fundamental and forgotten fact about America's Christian heritage: revival was not in its founding beginning a means to promote religion; it was the surprising result of a *critique* of religion' — religion being 'that self-assertion which presumes to be justified otherwise than by faith' (*America's Theologian*, p.63; emphasis in the original).
33. I owe several of these distinctions to Sam Shoemaker, *Extraordinary Living for Ordinary Men* (Grand Rapids: Zondervan, 1965), p.31.

but morality that is 'the greatest enemy of Christianity'.[34] Jesus did not come to start a new religion. He did not come to offer the best religion of all. He came to end all religion. The religious ethos currently inhaled by today's Westerners, to be nice and follow enough of the rules to appease God and others — what sociologist Christian Smith called 'moralistic therapeutic deism' — could not be further from the gospel.[35]

'Be good' Christianity is not wrong in the way that an artist painting a tree across the street and leaving out one of the branches is wrong, but in the way that such an artist would be wrong if he had been hired to paint the tree but had chopped it down instead. Moralistic Christianity is not incomplete Christianity; it is anti-Christianity.

'The last will be first.' It is those who recognize their need — who candidly admit they are 'last' regardless of when they were hired — who, strangely, are first. And it is those who regard themselves as 'first' who grumble (20:11) their way through this life and end up last in the sight of God.

Obedience from the heart

Sin, then, is not the problem. Sin exposes our need for the cross. Mechanized 'obedience' is the problem. Why? Because dutifully resolute obedience so naturally prevents our seeing the need for the cross. 'God is not hostile to sinners,' wrote

---

34. D. Martyn Lloyd-Jones, *Life in the Spirit in Marriage, Home and Work: An Exposition of Ephesians 5:18 to 6:9* (Grand Rapids: Baker, 1973), p.19.
35. Smith, *Soul Searching*, pp.162-63.

Luther, 'only to unbelievers.'[36]

To be sure, a follower of Christ who does not obey him is simply not a follower of Christ. Please hear me — *Christians obey*.

But we obey 'from the heart' (Rom. 6:17), not to help God's love for us, but in the light of God's love for us (2 Cor. 5:14; Eph. 5:2; 1 John 3:16). God's approval of us is reflected in, not strengthened by, our moral decisions. We must remember that Jesus was not essentially a sage but a herald. A sage proclaims the wisdom of healthy living, telling us what to do. A herald proclaims good news of victories won, telling what has been done.[37]

My family and I live in a part of the USA where flooded basements are a perennial problem due to the marshy ground on which the western suburbs of Chicago have been built. What happened to us with one such flooding is what often happens. The root tentacles of a large tree in our front yard had wound their way around the main pipe leading from our house to the city sewer. As those immensely strong tentacles began tasting moisture on the pipe, they slowly worked their way into the pipe itself, eventually filling the pipe with roots and sealing off all possibility for water to flow.

Every impulse of moral self-reflection in our heart; every smug thought of our own goodness; every self-contented consideration that we have left all to follow Jesus; every remembrance that we have 'borne the burden of the day and

---

36. Luther, *Luther's Works*, vol. 44, p.64.

37. See J. Gresham Machen, 'What is the Gospel?' in *J. Gresham Machen: Selected Shorter Writings*, ed. D. G. Hart (Phillipsburg, N.J.: Presbyterian & Reformed, 2004), pp.126-29.

the scorching heat' (20:12) — is one more root tentacle clogging the pipe of our heart through which God's forgiveness and our joy flow. Even such a subtle thing as gratitude that I am not a Pharisee can immediately turn me into one, since I am comparing my sin with the sin of another instead of with the holiness of God, before whom all claims of moral accomplishment die away.[38] Admission that we have a Pharisee in our heart, on the other hand, is to expose the moralism, bring it into the light and open the floodgates of healing.

This is the paradox of the gospel. As some have wisely said, then, there are not two kinds of people — the good and the bad, the obedient and the disobedient — but rather 'three kinds of men'.[39] In Christ, God offers a third kind of life that neither throws out the rules nor keeps the rules. It is no longer concerned with rules.

The foundation
The final and ultimate question, then, is how this can be so.

---

38. Noted by Luther, *Luther's Works*, vol. 51, p.17; Machen, *What is Faith?*, p.80.
39. The phrase is used for the same essential purpose by both F. B. Meyer, *The Directory of the Devout Life* (London: Morgan & Scott, 1904), pp.148-53, and C. S. Lewis, 'Three Kinds of Men,' in *Present Concerns* (London: Fount, 1986), pp.21-22. Similar are Søren Kierkegaard's three categories of living: aesthetic (living selfishly for one's own pleasure); ethical (living reluctantly in accordance with an external moral norm); and religious (living in the glad abandon of faith). See Clare Carlisle, *Kierkegaard: A Guide for the Perplexed* (London: Continuum, 2007), pp.77-83. Note that Kierkegaard's use of the word 'religion' is the polar opposite of the way in which I am employing that word.

How could it be that you and I become heirs of the world, perfectly approved before a sin-hating God, caught up in this great plan of setting straight a crooked world, solely by admitting that we don't deserve it? Here we come to the fourth and final reminder. Does what we have said here in this first section, about qualifying by simply refusing to try and qualify by one's own efforts, destroy the moral fabric of God's universe? Isn't this simply calling good bad and bad good? What about retaining some sense of right and wrong? Amid all this talk about God accepting the wicked so long as they confess their failure, what about God's *wrath* on the wicked?

The answer to this objection is the foundation for our entire reflection on the disobedient obedience of Matthew's Gospel.

On a little hill outside Jerusalem, where common thieves were strung up naked on crosses to die an excruciating death, Jesus Christ, sent by his Father for a specific purpose determined before the world began, gave himself up to be killed. On that hill, God poured out all his holy wrath on his beloved Son. This historical event is what maintains the moral fabric of the universe, so that you and I can be approved before God simply by admitting that we shouldn't be.

Just as the cross is the foundation for all that has been said here, so it is brought in at the very point in Matthew's Gospel where we left off. After telling his disciples the parable of the workers in the vineyard, Jesus gives them the fundamental reason *why* the generous landowner can be increasingly gracious in his dealings with every worker that is hired:

And as Jesus was going up to Jerusalem, he took the twelve disciples aside, and on the way he said to them, 'See, we are going up to Jerusalem. And the Son of Man will be delivered over to the chief priests and scribes, and they will condemn him to death and deliver him over to the Gentiles to be mocked and flogged and crucified, and he will be raised on the third day' (20:17-19).

Jesus died. That is the greatest surprise of all. On the cross, the one person who ever truly qualified allowed himself to be disqualified, so that you and I, naturally disqualified, can qualify — free of charge. The gospel is the happy invitation neither to trade in all our bad for being good, nor to trade in all our good for being better. The gospel invites us to trade in all our bad *and* our good for being free. Christianity's offer is not an invitation to become a Pharisee. It's an invitation to acknowledge the Pharisee who is already inside and to lay down our subtle efforts at appeasing God and others by our own resources.

Jesus died, and therefore all the bad we do can never lose God's love, yet all the good we do can never gain God's love. Jesus Christ is the only person to walk on this earth who truly deserved to be first, but he made himself last so that those who do nothing more than acknowledge that they are last can be first. To return one final time to the four passages in Matthew 19 – 20:

- The disciples' reaction to the children in 19:13–15 reminds us that we can have God's undivided attention without qualifying by our age or other social prerequisites, because on the cross Jesus allowed himself to be disqualified for us, to be rejected, not ultimately by his disciples, or even by the religious authorities, but by his own Father.

- The rich young man (19:16–22) teaches us that we can have eternal life without qualifying by law-keeping, because on the cross Jesus experienced hell despite living the only life that deserved heaven and being the only person who can truly say, 'All these have I kept.'

- The wrong assumptions of Peter and friends in 19:23–30 show us we can have a reward without qualifying by sacrifice, because on the cross Jesus made the ultimate sacrifice that means we can freely receive the ultimate reward.

- The workers who were hired (20:1–16) teach us about the fact that we can have a full day's wage without qualifying by doing comparatively more work than others, because Jesus worked the whole day, 'bearing the burden of the day', and then on the cross was denied any wage at all.

With Jesus, morality is not what we think it is. Because he died and rose again, our disobedience can be compensated not by our efforts but by receiving his efforts in his self-emptying faith. If we try to use our obedience as some sort of compensation, it becomes disobedience.

This is surprising. The disciples were slow to grasp the point; so are you and I. But Jesus died even for that. All is taken care of. We are free to be fully and irreversibly forgiven. Recognize that you don't deserve it, look to him, and you are in.

PART 2 – MARK:
THE SURPRISE OF THE KING
AS A CRIMINAL

4.

THE SURPRISE OF JESUS'
MISSION

'EVERYTHING ABOUT GOD is so completely different from what we thought or feared,' wrote German theologian Helmut Thielicke half a century ago.[40] This is precisely what we find in each of the four Gospels. Each account, in its own way, disabuses us of our natural, tame intuitions about who Jesus is and what it means to be his disciple.

The deepest surprise built into the fabric of the Gospel of Mark lies not primarily in the realm of what it means to be a truly obedient follower of Jesus, but deals rather with Jesus himself (though, as we will see, the two are closely linked). Jesus' *definition of morality* is counterintuitive in Matthew; Jesus' *own mission* is counterintuitive in Mark. For in Mark, we see most clearly the surprise of the king being

---

40. Helmut Thielicke, *The Waiting Father: Sermons on the Parables of Jesus*, trans. John W. Doberstein (New York: Harper & Row, 1959), p.29.

treated as a criminal — or as Jonathan Edwards put it, the lion being treated as a sacrificial lamb. Yet through his lamb-like slaughter, Christ himself is shown to be the greatest of lions.

> Christ appeared ... as both a lion and a lamb. He appeared as a lamb in the hands of his cruel enemies; as a lamb in the paws, and between the devouring jaws, of a roaring lion; yea, he was a lamb actually slain by this lion: and yet at the same time, as the Lion of the tribe of Judah, he conquers and triumphs over Satan, destroying his own devourer.[41]

We will see this startling conjunction of the highest majesty with the most despicable fate by taking a passage from Mark and reading it against the backdrop of the Gospel as a whole. The passage we will zero in on is Mark 8:22-38. When we come to John's Gospel we will once more concentrate our attention on Jesus himself, but there the focus will be on *who Jesus is* (his person); here in Mark it will be on *what Jesus did* (his work).

The regal Son of Man

The Gospel of Mark falls neatly into two halves. The first half (1:1 – 8:30) shows us Jesus the king. The second half (8:31 –

---

41. Jonathan Edwards, 'The Excellency of Christ,' in *Sermons and Discourses, 1734–1738, The Works of Jonathan Edwards, vol. 19*, ed. M. X. Lesser (New Haven: Yale University Press, 2001), p.580. G. K. Chesterton, in his own inimitable way, notes the paradoxical combination of the metaphors of the lion and the lamb in Christianity (*Orthodoxy*; New York: John Lane, 1908, pp.180-81).

16:8) shows us Jesus increasingly hurtling towards the fate of a criminal. The hinge on which this transition takes place is Mark 8:22-38.

To begin with, let's be clear about the way the first half of Mark depicts Jesus as a king. How do we see this? In two ways: first, by the way Jesus refers to himself; and, secondly, by the way Mark structures the broader flow of his narrative.

First, consider *the way Jesus refers to himself*. By far the most common title Jesus takes to himself is 'Son of Man'. It is found thirteen times in Mark, including once at the end of the passage on which we are focusing (8:38). What is the significance of Jesus referring to himself in this way? Often it is assumed that the title underscores Jesus' humanity — he is a son of man in that he is a real flesh-and-blood human being. This may certainly be implied. After all, Scripture often uses the phrase 'son of man' to refer to one who is a mere mortal (for example, Ps. 8:4; Ezek. 2:1).

Centrally, however, on the lips of Jesus in the Gospels, the title 'Son of Man' means almost exactly the opposite. Scholars generally agree that Jesus takes this title from Daniel 7. Here we read of a vision given to Daniel, which Daniel describes as follows:

As I looked,
thrones were placed,
        and the Ancient of Days took his seat;
his clothing was white as snow,
        and the hair of his head like pure wool;

71

his throne was fiery flames;

    its wheels were burning fire.

A stream of fire issued

    and came out from before him;

a thousand thousands served him,

    and ten thousand times ten thousand stood before him;

 the court sat in judgment,

    and the books were opened ...

and behold, with the clouds of heaven

    there came one like a son of man,

and he came to the Ancient of Days

    and was presented before him.

And to him was given dominion

    and glory and a kingdom,

that all peoples, nations, and languages

    should serve him;

his dominion is an everlasting dominion,

    which shall not pass away,

and his kingdom one

    that shall not be destroyed (Dan. 7:9-10, 13-14).

Jesus probably has Daniel 7 in mind when he refers to himself as the Son of Man because elsewhere he draws on other elements of Daniel 7 when referring to himself with this title. For instance, in Mark 13:26, Jesus tells his disciples that 'they will see the Son of Man coming in clouds with great power and glory' (cf. Matt. 24:30). In Mark 14:62, similarly, the high priest asks Jesus whether he is the Messiah.[42] Jesus responds, 'I am, and you will see the Son of Man seated at the right hand of Power, and coming with the clouds of heaven' (cf. Matt. 26:64). In such passages, while referring to himself as the Son of Man, Jesus also draws on other language from Daniel 7.

What is striking to notice in all this is that this son of man in Daniel's vision is anything but a mere mortal. He is a king, a king so regal that he possesses marks of the divine. On the one hand, the son of man is presented *to* the Ancient of Days (God), indicating that the son of man is distinct from the Ancient of Days. Yet this son of man receives what can only be given to one who is divine: 'dominion and glory ... that all peoples, nations, and languages should serve him' (Dan. 7:14). In Mark 8:38, moreover, Jesus speaks of the Son of Man coming 'in the glory of his Father' — evidently, then, the Son of Man is also the Son of God.[43] Moreover, his rule will last forever: 'his dominion is an everlasting dominion, which shall not pass away' (Dan. 7:14). No merely human king can rule forever.

---

42. Mark 14:61 uses the word 'Christ' (*Christos*), the Greek equivalent to the Hebrew term *Meshiach*. We thus get our English term 'Christ' from the Greek word for the Messiah, and our English word 'Messiah' from the Hebrew term for the same figure.

43. See Seyoon Kim's extensive treatment of this in his 'The "Son of Man" as the Son of God' (WUNT 30; Tübingen: Mohr Siebeck, 1983); on Mark 8:38, see p.1. For a more accessible overview to Mark, see the useful introduction by Joel F. Williams in *What the New Testament Authors Really Cared About: A Survey of their Writings*, ed. Kenneth Berding and Matt Williams (Grand Rapids: Kregel, 2008), pp.44-57.

When we read in Mark, then, that 'the Son of Man has authority on earth to forgive sins' (2:10), or that 'the Son of Man is lord even of the Sabbath' (2:28), we are seeing Jesus identify himself as the awaited ruler, the hope of Jewish expectations, the king whose identity whispers nothing less than the divine.[44]

When Messiah came, tyranny would end. There would be no more Roman oppression, no more forced pagan sacrifices. All would be put right. Israel would regain its place as God's chosen nation, to which the peoples of the earth would stream (Isa. 2:2-4; Micah 4:1-2).

Portrait of a king

Jesus' kingly status is even more clearly seen when we step back and take stock of the broader flow of the narrative in Mark's Gospel and the way it falls cleanly into two halves. The first half in particular (1:1 – 8:30) establishes Jesus as the long-awaited king, the Messiah, and does so in a way that is not particularly surprising. He is well received. And why shouldn't he be? This is the long-anticipated deliverer.

Flipping briefly through the opening eight chapters, we find a rapidly unfolding account of Jesus' ministry with a consistently (if not exclusively) glowing depiction of Jesus, his ministry, and his reception by the masses.

- The first verse of the book announces that Jesus Christ is 'the Son of God' (1:1); while this probably hints at

---

44. See Douglas W. Kinnard, *Messiah Jesus: Christology in His Day and Ours* (New York: Peter Lang, 2008), pp.401-2.

Jesus' divinity, the title primarily refers to the expected ruler from the line of David, the Messiah, who would wipe out Israel's enemies and reign forever on David's throne.[45] Jesus is, moreover, called 'Christ' here, a Greek word meaning 'anointed one', the Messiah-King.

- John the Baptist, the most famous and powerful preacher of the day ('all the country of Judea and all Jerusalem were going out to him', 1:5), prepares for Jesus by saying that 'After me comes he who is mightier than I' (1:7).

- God the Father himself underscores Jesus' exalted status a few lines later when Jesus comes to be baptized: 'You are my beloved Son; with you I am well pleased' (1:11).

- The members of the synagogue 'were astonished at his teaching, for he taught them as one who had authority' (1:22).

- Upon his healing a man with an unclean (demonic) spirit at the synagogue, the onlookers 'were all amazed' (1:27).

- Jesus' reputation is not slow in gathering force: halfway through the first chapter of Mark, we read that 'his fame spread everywhere throughout all the surrounding region of Galilee' (1:28).

- After he had left the synagogue and healed Peter's mother-in-law, 'they brought to him all who were sick or oppressed by demons. And the whole city was gathered together at the door' (1:32-33).

---

45. See 2 Sam. 7:12-16; Ps. 2:7; Isa. 9:6-7; Jer. 23:5-6; 33:14-26; Acts 13:32-34.

- Continuing to preach throughout Galilee, he was repeatedly welcomed into the synagogues (1:39). 'Jesus could no longer openly enter a town,' Mark tells us, 'and people were coming to him from every quarter' (1:45).

Mark paints a radiant portrait — and that is just the first chapter! Right from the start, he drives home the regal reception with which Jesus is welcomed by the masses. The Old Testament promised that a royal son of man, who would receive 'dominion and glory and a kingdom', would rule in 'an everlasting dominion' (Dan. 7:14). One would come who would 'bring good news to the poor … bind up the broken-hearted … proclaim liberty to the captives' (Isa. 61:1). Jesus himself was the fulfilment of these ancient hopes and longings.[46] Mark wants us to see this.

The rest of the first half of Mark continues similarly. While clusters of grouchy religious authorities are occasionally bothered by Jesus' acts of mercy, his general magnetism snowballs through Mark 1 – 8.

- Jesus not only heals a paralytic but forgives his sins, and 'they were all amazed and glorified God, saying, "We never saw anything like this!"' (2:12).

- Jesus declares that he is 'lord even of the Sabbath' (2:28).

- When he withdraws to the sea with his disciples, 'a great crowd followed', forcing Jesus into a boat 'lest they crush him' (3:7, 9).

---

46. See also Luke 4:16-21.

- After calling the twelve apostles, Jesus seeks to return home, but 'the crowd gathered again, so that they could not even eat' (3:20).

- Chapter 4 opens with (yet again) 'a very large crowd gathered about him', so that Jesus is once more forced to teach from a boat pushed a little way out from the shore (4:1).

- Shortly afterwards, Jesus silences a storm with a mere word, prompting his trembling disciples to wonder aloud, 'Who then is this, that even the wind and the sea obey him?' (4:41).

- In Mark 5, Jesus heals a demon-possessed man who, having run to Jesus and fallen down before him (5:6), plainly recognizes Jesus to be the 'Son of the Most High God' (5:7), and when the account of what Jesus had done is relayed to others, 'everyone marveled' (5:20).

- The rest of Mark 5 describes Jesus healing a woman suffering from a physical problem by the simple act of her touching him (5:24-34), and then raising a synagogue ruler's daughter from the dead by a mere word — upon which those present 'were immediately overcome with amazement' (5:42).

- In Mark 6, the response to continued teaching in the synagogue by Jesus is that 'many who heard him were astonished, saying, "Where did this man get these things? What is the wisdom given to him?"' (6:2).

- Soon afterwards, Jesus feeds five thousand men, plus many more women and children (6:30-44).

- He then walks on water and, upon his entering the disciples' boat, the strong wind that had come up dies down, 'and they were utterly astounded' (6:51).

- Mark 6 concludes: 'And wherever he came, in villages, cities, or countryside, they laid the sick in the marketplaces and implored him that they might touch even the fringe of his garment. And as many as touched it were made well' (6:56).

- In Mark 7, after Jesus has rebuked the Pharisees' overly scrupulous dietary habits (7:14-23) and has healed, first, the daughter of a Gentile woman, and then a deaf man (7:24-36), the chapter ends with Mark describing the way those around Jesus 'were astonished beyond measure' (7:37).

- In Mark 8, Jesus feeds four thousand (8:1-21).

Awe upon awe! All through the first eight chapters of Mark, Jesus heals, performs miracles, casts out demons, calms storms, forgives sins, raises the dead — in a word, 'He has done all things well' (7:37). Time and again those gathered are 'astonished', 'amazed', and filled with reverent wonder at this one who had come among them. This is Jesus the Lord, the King. This is the Christ to whom waves of onlookers are drawn.

However, it is not a full portrait of Jesus' mission. Yes, Israel's king had landed, healing the sick, raising the dead, restoring the broken. But that was only half the mission.

The pinnacle of Mark

All this brings us to the middle of Mark 8. We pick up the story at the closing of the feeding of the four thousand:

> And they came to Bethsaida. And some people brought to him a blind man and begged him to touch him. And he took the blind man by the hand and led him out of the village, and when he had spat on his eyes and laid his hands on him, he asked him, 'Do you see anything?' And he looked up and said, 'I see men, but they look like trees, walking.' Then Jesus laid his hands on his eyes again; and he opened his eyes, his sight was restored, and he saw everything clearly. And he sent him to his home, saying, 'Do not even enter the village.'

> And Jesus went on with his disciples to the villages of Caesarea Philippi. And on the way he asked his disciples, 'Who do people say that I am?' And they told him, 'John the Baptist; and others say, Elijah; and others, one of the prophets.' And he asked them, 'But who do you say that I am?' Peter answered him, 'You are the Christ.' And he strictly charged them to tell no one about him.

> And he began to teach them that the Son of Man must suffer many things and be rejected by the elders and the chief priests and the scribes and be killed, and after three days rise again. And he said this plainly. And Peter took him aside and began to rebuke him. But

turning and seeing his disciples, he rebuked Peter and said, 'Get behind me, Satan! For you are not setting your mind on the things of God, but on the things of man' (8:22-33).

What's going on here?

We have three short accounts stacked up next to one another. A blind man is healed; Peter boldly confesses that Jesus is the Christ, the Messiah-King; and Jesus announces his impending suffering and death, refuting in the strongest terms Peter's resistance to this suffering. The three accounts mutually interpret one another.

The moment at which Peter proclaims, 'You are the Christ', is the point at which the disciples have been won over to see that Jesus is the coming king they have so long anticipated. This confession is the conclusion to which all of Mark 1 – 8 has been driving. It has taken seven complete chapters and thirty verses of chapter 8, and the disciples are finally convinced. This is the high point of Mark.

Yet it is here, halfway through the Gospel, that the whole account swivels around and begins moving in the opposite direction.[47] For this is only half of what the disciples need to see. They see that he is the king — and if he is the king they have been expecting, that would be enough. However, if he is not the king they expect, but the king they most deeply need — if he has come not to deal with their circumstances, but with their sins — then something more is needed. This aspect

---

47. See Jeremias, *Rediscovering the Parables*, p.172.

of Jesus' mission the disciples have not yet grasped.

And this is what the healing of the blind man in two stages, an account told only in Mark, is showing us. Jesus 'dealt with the blind man as he did', preached Martyn Lloyd-Jones, 'in order to enable the disciples to see themselves as they were'.[48]

Teaching by healing

Throughout the Gospels Jesus ministers in two ways: teaching and healing. This is the only place in all four Gospels where the two are rolled into one so that the healing *is* the teaching. Why did Jesus heal this blind man in two steps? Was he unable to do it in one fell swoop? That explanation is hardly satisfactory when we are talking about someone who raised the dead with a brief uttered word (5:41-42) or healed the sick from a distance (Matt. 8:5-13).

No, by healing this blind man in two stages Jesus is not only healing the man but teaching the disciples. In a single event he is giving the blind man mercy and giving his disciples a mirror. Halfway through his healing, the blind man did not yet have 20/20 vision; halfway through Mark's Gospel, the disciples do not yet have 20/20 vision. They understand Jesus' mission, but only fuzzily. When Peter announces, 'You are the Christ' (8:29), he is, in the flow of Mark, asserting spiritually what the blind man had just asserted physically: 'I see men, but they look like trees, walking' (8:24).

---

48. Lloyd-Jones, *Spiritual Depression*, p.39. This statement comes in a sermon on Mark 8:22-26.

The disciples had been convinced that Jesus was the coming king. But the *kind* of king he would be still eluded them. Their natural intuitions, and ours, perceive power and triumph to be the way in which God's climactic redemptive purposes in the world unfurl. This is why Peter responded in the way he did to the thought of Jesus' death in verse 32: 'Peter took him aside and began to rebuke him.' If you and I had been there we would doubtless have endorsed Peter's very sensible admonition.

Jesus would have none of it. To the astonishment of his followers the Son of Man announces, halfway through Mark's Gospel, that he is *not* going to be received by the Bible scholars of the day and make the Romans suffer, but that he is going to be rejected by the Bible scholars of the day and that the Romans will make him suffer.

It is around this point, of Peter's confession and Jesus' response, that the whole Gospel of Mark pivots. This is the hinge.[49] The disciples now see that Jesus is the king, but do not see that he will take the way of the criminal. They see that he is the lion, but not that he will be treated as a lamb. Their vision, like that of the blind man half-healed, is blurry. They see that Jesus is the Messiah, but not that he must be a suffering Messiah. They see that he is the son of man prophesied in Daniel, but not that the way to the throne of 'everlasting dominion' (Dan. 7:14) is through a cross that the

---

49. See Richard Bauckham, *Jesus and the God of Israel: God Crucified and Other Studies on the New Testament's Christology of Divine Identity* (Grand Rapids: Eerdmans, 2008), pp.262-63.

road to the highest mountaintop is through the deepest valley. After the victorious announcement of verse 29, the rest of Mark's Gospel is a slow descent into ignominious suffering and death.

The first half of Mark shows *that* Jesus is the king. The second half of Mark shows *how* Jesus is the king.

A Servant King

Several times throughout Mark, Jesus explicitly announces his impending suffering to his disciples. Yet notice that none of these warnings occurs in the first eight chapters, the chapters of wonder-filled 'amazement' and 'astonishment'. They begin immediately after Jesus elicits from his disciples the confident assertion from spokesman Peter: 'You are the Christ' (8:29).

Three times in chapters 8 – 10, beginning in the immediate wake of Peter's assured confession of Jesus as the Messiah, Jesus speaks of his imminent suffering and death (8:31; 9:30-31; 10:32-34; see also 9:12). Narry Santos's book on servanthood in the Gospel of Mark calls these the three 'paradoxical discourses' because they combine (rather than set at odds) the greatest of authority with the lowest of servanthood.[50] It is none other than the triumphant Son of Man who will suffer in this way. And in each of these three paradoxical discourses,

50. Narry F. Santos, *Slave of All: The Paradox of Authority and Servanthood in the Gospel of Mark* (Journal for the Society of New Testament Studies Supplement Series 237; London: Sheffield Academic Press, 2003), pp.58-59, 144-47. Note the title of T. Desmond Alexander's study of the 'king' theme throughout the whole Bible: *The Servant King: The Bible's Portrait of the Messiah* (Vancouver: Regent College Publishing, 2003).

Jesus' prediction is met with incomprehension and resistance on the part of the disciples (8:32-33; 9:32; 10:35-37). Then in chapter 11 Jesus makes his entry into Jerusalem, as the remainder of Mark hurtles towards the events of Passion Week when Jesus is arrested and crucified. One way in which we see that Peter and the disciples did not understand both sides of Jesus' mission — the noble and the ignoble — is that, despite Peter's bold confession at the close of the first half of Mark (8:29), the second half of Mark ironically closes with a pagan centurion confessing Jesus as the Son of God (15:39), while Peter denies him (14:66-72).

Jesus did not begin his ministry with the unavoidable ignominy awaiting him. He began by winning over the disciples to the fact that he was indeed the Messiah. All the simmering anticipations of coming liberation were culminating in this carpenter from Nazareth. But he is not the kind of Messiah they expected. This is the reason for the numerous times in the first half of Mark that Jesus instructs those whom he has healed to keep quiet about what he has done (1:34, 43-44; 3:12; 5:43; 7:36; 8:30). New Testament scholar Craig Blomberg explains that Jesus 'was very cautious about accepting the title or allowing premature enthusiasm to overwhelm his mission because popular Christological expectation did not leave room for a *suffering* Messiah'.[51] As soon as Jesus has won his disciples over, he begins to deconstruct and then reconstruct

---

51. Craig L. Blomberg, *Jesus and the Gospels: An Introduction and Survey* (Nashville: Broadman & Holman, 2nd edition, 2009), p.133 (emphasis in the original).

their understanding of what kind of Messiah he must be if the disciples are to be part of God's kingdom. He must suffer as a common criminal.[52]

Strikingly, the Greek word for the Messiah, *Christos*, from which we get our English word 'Christ', occurs in the first verse of Mark and then does not reappear until Peter's confession in 8:29; yet it appears six times in the remaining chapters, which make up the half of Mark's Gospel that highlights Jesus' suffering.[53] And in all three major predictions of his impending suffering in Mark 8 – 10, Jesus identifies himself as the Son of Man, hijacking the title belonging to the conquering king of Daniel 7. In these ways a scandalous paradox unfolds as Mark indicates that Jesus' status as the coming Christ and the reigning Son of Man is not in competition with his path of suffering. On the contrary, it is *through* suffering that Jesus seals his status as the heavenly Son of Man, receiving all glory from the Father and ruling for evermore (cf. Phil. 2:6-11).[54]

Not only would he suffer, he would be rejected. A martyr Messiah, suffering before the people and lauded for his suffering, would be difficult enough. Jesus experienced something far worse: 'The Son of Man must suffer many things *and be rejected…*' (8:31). Dietrich Bonhoeffer comments:

52. See Hans K. LaRondelle, *The Israel of God in Prophecy: Principles of Prophetic Interpretation* (Berrien Springs, Mich.: Andrews University Press, 1983), p.95.
53. See Blomberg, *Jesus and the Gospels*, p.132.
54. See Bauckham, *Jesus and the God of Israel*, p.55; Adela Y. Collins and John J. Collins, *King and Messiah as Son of God: Divine, Human, and Angelic Messianic Figures in Biblical and Related Literature* (Grand Rapids: Eerdmans, 2008), p.150.

Had he only suffered, Jesus might still have been applauded as the Messiah. All the sympathy and admiration of the world might have been focused on his passion. It could have been viewed as a tragedy with its own intrinsic value, dignity and honor. But in the passion Jesus is a rejected Messiah... Suffering and rejection sum up the whole cross of Jesus.[55]

And by whom would he be rejected? By the hostile Roman overlords? 'The Son of Man must suffer many things and be rejected by the elders and the chief priests and the scribes' (8:31). Jesus was to be despised and shunned by the Jewish authorities, the very ones who ought to have embraced him. It was those with the best theology, not the worst, who rejected the Son of God.

Surprising Old Testament fulfilments

When he hung on the cross, Jesus was experiencing what the Old Testament considered to be the ultimate curse, the epitome of a repulsive, feared fate, the fate reserved for the worst criminals: 'And if a man has committed a crime punishable by death and he is put to death, and you hang him on a tree, his body shall not remain all night on the tree, but you shall bury him the same day, for a hanged man is cursed by God' (Deut. 21:22-23). According to Israelite law, the worst crimes called for the worst punishment, the punishment that

---

55. Dietrich Bonhoeffer, *The Cost of Discipleship*, trans. R. H. Fuller (New York: Touchstone, 1995), pp.86-87.

was considered to rest under the very curse of God — being hung up on a tree.

Yet this criminal fate, according to the New Testament writers, is exactly what Jesus experienced. 'Christ redeemed us from the curse of the law,' wrote Paul, 'by becoming a curse for us, for it is written, "Cursed is everyone who is hanged on a tree"' (Gal. 3:13, quoting Deut. 21:23). 'He himself bore our sins in his body on the tree' (1 Peter 2:24).

Before and after this passage in 1 Peter 2, Peter alludes several times to Isaiah 53. Here Isaiah speaks enigmatically of a coming 'servant' who would suffer vicariously for the sins of his people. Bringing together Deuteronomy 21, Isaiah 53, Galatians 3, and 1 Peter 2, we find that the shocking disclosure of the New Testament is that when the Old Testament spoke in some places of a coming triumphant Son of Man and when it spoke in other places of a coming Suffering Servant, these predictions, seemingly polar opposites, are realized *in the same person*.[56]

The disciples wanted liberation. But they were short-sighted. They wanted liberation from their circumstances — Roman occupation, pagan overlords, Israel's internationally undervalued reputation. But Jesus had come truly to liberate them. He had come to liberate them from their sins. He came to free them not from others, but from themselves — not from the overlords of Rome, but from the overlord of sin (Rom. 6:14).

---

56. See Herman Ridderbos, *Paul and Jesus: Origin and General Character of Paul's Preaching of Christ*, trans. David H. Freeman (Philadelphia: Presbyterian & Reformed, 1958), p.31.

For this blessed reason the Gospel of Mark does not end at Mark 8:30. Jesus' mission was not just that of a lion. Circumstantial liberation required a kingly Messiah, and a kingly Messiah alone. Spiritual liberation — real liberation — required a kingly Messiah who would himself be bound like a criminal so that his followers could be liberated in the only sense that ultimately matters.

Jesus the king would suffer as a common criminal. Magnificence would be turned inside out. This is the surprise of Mark. Jonathan Edwards rightly preached that in Jesus there is 'an admirable conjunction ... of infinite dignity, and infinite condescension and love to the infinitely unworthy'.[57]

---

57. Edwards, 'The Excellency of Christ,' p.579.

5.

JESUS' CROSS-BEARING CALL

THE HEALING IN two stages of the blind man's physical vision, then, was a tangible picture of the two-staged healing of the disciples' blindness regarding how their Lord's mission would unfold. And Mark shows us the surprise of Jesus' mission — the king, the long-awaited Son of Man, dies as a common criminal.

The surprise of Christian discipleship
Yet Jesus does not leave the spotlight on himself in responding to his disciples' wayward understanding of his mission. Immediately after rebuking Peter, Jesus turns to those nearby and reveals to them what it means to be led by a suffering Messiah-King: 'If anyone would come after me, let him deny himself and take up his cross and follow me. For whoever would save his life will lose it, but whoever loses his life for my sake and the gospel's will save it' (8:34-35).

For disciples of Jesus, the Messiah's death not only plucks them from the easy path to hell, but also places them on the hard path to heaven. 'When Christ calls a man,' wrote Bonhoeffer, 'he bids him come and die.'[58]

Jesus' suffering was ultimately so that we would not suffer forever. The greatest accomplishment of Jesus' mission is something he did on our behalf — vicarious atonement. But Jesus was not only a substitute. He was also a pioneer (Heb. 2:10; 12:2). He not only bears the cross in our place, he also blazes a cross-shaped trail that we are to follow. The suffering of Christ not only wins us forgiveness, but trains us to lose our lives for his sake — as we learn to deny ourselves, take up our cross and follow him.

Followers of Jesus trade in temporal pleasures with eternal suffering for temporal suffering with eternal pleasures. These are our only two options. C. S. Lewis echoed the teaching of Mark when he said that 'a crucifixion of the natural self is the passport to everlasting life. Nothing that has not died will be resurrected.'[59] Meaningful discipleship under Jesus Christ is not the fruit of cool, detached onlooking, however appreciative of his teaching one may be. Only the disciple who loses his life for Jesus' sake, and thereby secures the only life worth having, truly understands who Jesus is and how God's redemptive purposes in the world operate — not only through his Son, but also through his people.

---

58. Bonhoeffer, *The Cost of Discipleship*, p.89.
59. C. S. Lewis, 'Membership,' in *The Weight of Glory and Other Addresses* (New York: Touchstone, 1996), p.129.

Notice that Jesus does not call us to allow ourselves to be denied by some outside agent; he does not call us to be ready to have a cross placed upon us; he does not call us to wander after him. He calls us to deny ourselves, take up our cross, and follow him. Proactive exertion, not passive compliance, is the *modus operandi* of vital Christian discipleship.

Henry Scougal was professor of divinity at Aberdeen University until his death in 1678 at the age of twenty-eight. The year before he died Scougal wrote a letter to a distraught friend in which he said:

Never doth a soul know what solid joy and substantial pleasure is, till once, being weary of itself, it renounce all propriety, give itself up unto the Author of its being, and feel itself become a hallowed and devoted thing, and can say, I am content to be anything for him, and care not for myself, but that I may serve him.[60]

To take up the cross is to take up joy — painful joy, but real joy. For to take up the cross is to walk with the one who in great love bore the ultimate cross in our place. Aim at joy, and you will miss it. Aim at Christ, and his cross-bearing call, and you will find it.

Contrary as it is to all our presuppositions, the way to save our life is to lose it. Death was the way to life for Jesus. Death is the way to life for Jesus' disciples. 'Die before you die. There

---

60. Henry Scougal, *The Life of God in the Soul of Man* (Fearn, Scotland: Christian Focus, 1996), p.76.

is no chance after,' remarks a character in C. S. Lewis's *Till We Have Faces*.[61]

If we tunnel into the very heart of Christian discipleship as articulated by Mark, we find, echoing the mission of Jesus himself, this startling principle: loss is gain. Death is life. Yielding all guarantees; receiving all. Self-denial for the sake of the gospel is the secret to saving our life. This was the way the upside-down mission of Jesus worked out, and it is the path of discipleship for his people.[62] Glad abandon is our only sanity.

Contrary to what all our instincts of self-preservation whisper to us every day, abandonment to Jesus is the safest investment we can make. Our only security is renunciation of all that this world holds secure.

---

61. C. S. Lewis, *Till We Have Faces: A Myth Retold* (New York: Harcourt, 1956), p.279. See also Luther, *Luther's Works*, vol. 51, p.25, note 3.

62. Reflecting on Mark 10:45, Schlatter writes, 'He makes of himself a ransom and makes his own death the deed that frees the condemned. Out of his royal sending comes service, and out of his service, which makes him the last and humbles him beneath everyone else, arises his glory. In this the disciples can recognize how one becomes great in God's kingdom' (Schlatter, *Do We Know Jesus?*, p.339).

6.

BROKEN AND BLIND SINNERS

THE EMOTIONAL CASH value of heeding Christ's call to
follow him is the realization that taking up our cross is not an
alternative to joy. Cross-bearing is not masochism. The grim
self-denial to which Jesus calls us in Mark 8 does not quench,
but fans, the flames of the irrepressible gladness in which
we have been swept up. We are not called to be sorrowful *or*
rejoicing, but both (2 Cor. 6:10); not self-denying *or* joyful,
but both.

Triumphant brokenness

One way we see Christians falling off on one side or the other
of this tension is in the encouragement of some that believers
should be perpetually 'broken', on the one hand, and in the
call to 'triumphant' or 'victorious' Christian living, on the
other hand. Both amount to one-sided reductionism of a
gospel-formed life.

Are Christians to be broken? Well, it depends what we mean. If by 'broken' we mean downcast, long-faced, perpetually discouraged, handwringing, abject, ever grieving over sins — no. If by 'broken' we mean contrite, low before the Lord, poignantly aware of personal weakness, self-divesting, able to laugh at ourselves, having sober judgment, being sensitive to the depths of sin within us — yes.

Are Christians to be triumphant? If by 'triumphant' we mean self-assured, superficial, obtuse to personal weakness, beyond correction, self-confident, quick to diagnose others' weaknesses and our own strengths, showy, triumphalistic — no. If by 'triumphant' we mean confident of God's unconquerable purposes in the world through faltering disciples, bold with a boldness that accords with the outrageous promises of the Bible, quietly abandoning ourselves to God in the light of Christ's irrepressible victory, relentless in reminding the enemy of Christ's emptying of the power of Satan's accusations, prepared to take risks not for the sake of reputation-seeking but fueled by a faith that is fixated on God — yes.

Brokenness without triumph is Eeyorish gloom that emphasizes the Fall to the neglect of redemption, crucifixion to the neglect of resurrection, and Mark 9 – 16 to the neglect of Mark 1 – 8. It is personally *under-realized* eschatology. Triumph without brokenness is Buzz Lightyear-ish naïveté that emphasizes redemption to the neglect of the Fall, resurrection to the neglect of crucifixion, Mark 1 – 8 to the neglect of Mark 9 – 16.[63] It is personally *over-realized* eschatology. 'Cross and

63. Eeyore is the gloomy, misanthropic donkey in A. A. Milne's *Winnie the*

crown, death and resurrection, humiliation and exaltation lie on the same line,' wrote Dutch theologian Herman Bavinck.[64] Our two options are: a cross with a crown, or neither; contrite brokenness with ultimate triumph, or neither — not one or the other. For in the gospel we are liberated to experience *both* Fall *and* redemption, crucifixion *and* resurrection, brokenness *and* triumph, Mark 1 – 8 *and* Mark 9 – 16. This is so because the only person who was ever in himself triumphant without brokenness switched places with those who in themselves are only broken without triumph, so that now the greatest triumph is freely ours, even as brokenness remains.

While brokenness is not the final word for Christians — there is no brokenness in the first two chapters of the Bible and none in the final two chapters — any seasoned saint can attest that the strange way God brings us to treasure this triumph is *through*, not by circumventing, present brokenness. For this reason we find scattered throughout all four Gospels numerous aphorisms from the mouth of Jesus that pithily crystallize the upside-down truth that bearing the brokenness of the cross and the triumph of glory are not mutually exclusive. The cross and the glory are bound up with one another. Glory comes, for us as for our Lord, through the cross. It is in losing our lives that we find them (Matt. 10:39; cf. Luke 17:33). Humbling

---

Pooh; Buzz Lightyear is the naïve, over-optimistic space explorer in the *Toy Story* movies.

64. Herman Bavinck, *Reformed Dogmatics*, ed. John Bolt; trans. John Vriend (Grand Rapids: Baker, 4 vols., 2003 2008), vol. 4, p.423. 'If we will not carry the cross,' writes J. C. Ryle, 'we shall never wear the crown' (J. C. Ryle, *Ryle's Expository Thoughts on the Gospels: Mark*; Grand Rapids: Zondervan, p.169).

oneself like a child is true greatness (Matt. 18:1-4; cf. Luke 9:23-24, 48). The last will be first and the first last (Matt. 19:30; 20:16; cf. Mark 10:31; Luke 13:30). Those seeking to be great must serve others (Matt. 20:26-28; cf. Mark 9:35; 10:43-45). The kingdom of God is like a mustard seed, a tiny seed that nevertheless provides the largest, most shady branches (4:30-32). The humble will be exalted and the self-exalting humbled (Luke 14:11; cf. Luke 16:15; 18:14). It is the grain of wheat that falls into the ground and dies that bears much fruit (John 12:24-25).

The fierce impulse bubbling up within every one of us as we roll out of bed in the morning is to seek glory (triumph) and avoid a cross (brokenness). In Mark 8, Jesus presents us with a choice: glory now and a cross forever, or a cross now and glory forever.[65] Jesus went to the cross, however, so that when you and I deliberately take up our cross, it becomes a means of life — 'whoever loses his life … will save it'. And this is possible because Jesus went to the cross when he *didn't* deserve it.

In the first half of Mark's Gospel, then, we see Jesus as the king. In the second half, we see him preparing for, and then experiencing, the suffering and death of a criminal. In the

---

65. Francis Schaeffer wrote, 'Christ taught His disciples that they were not to be called "Rabbi" or "Master" (Matt. 23:8, 10) and that the greatest among them would be the servant of all (Mark 10:44). Doesn't each one of us tend to reverse this, following our natural inclination as fallen men while ignoring the Word of God? Don't we like the foremost place? … Scripture is clear that we must either humble ourselves now or be humbled in the future… If [a Christian] has not humbled himself in this life, he will be humbled then. There is no third way' (Francis Schaeffer, *No Little People*, Wheaton: Crossway, 2003, pp.68-69, 70).

first half Jesus wins our submission; in the second half he wins our hearts.

In the first half of Mark we learn that God has come to us; in the second half, we learn that we can come to God.

Blind seeing and seeing blindness

Stepping back and viewing Mark 8 in the flow of Mark's Gospel as a whole, we have noticed that the disciples saw Jesus' kingly status in Mark 1 – 8 but did not yet see what kind of king he would be. This emphasis on 'seeing' occurs not only in the healing of the blind man, but is pervasive throughout Mark 8 – 10.

For instance, Jesus asks his disciples in 8:18, 'Having eyes do you not see?' Shortly afterwards he performs the two-staged healing of the blind man, with an explicit focus throughout on seeing. In 9:1 Jesus tells the crowd gathered round that 'there are some standing here who will not taste death until they see the kingdom of God after it has come with power'.[66] References to seeing multiply throughout chapter 9 and into chapter 10.[67] The vision/blindness motif then culminates in another healing of blindness, that of Bartimaeus (10:46-52), which probably joins with the two-staged healing of Mark 8 to form a pair of bookends around Jesus' three declarations of suffering and death in Mark 8 – 10.

---

66. It is likely that this cryptic statement refers to the transfiguration, which is recounted immediately afterwards (Mark 9:2-13). Note 2 Peter 1:16-18, which, in describing the transfiguration from Peter's point of view, speaks of it in terms of 'coming' and 'power' (v. 16), just as Mark 9:1 does.
67. Mark 9:8, 14, 15, 20, 38, 47; 10:14, 21, 23, 27, 33.

We are drawing out the seeing/blindness theme here because at the end of chapter 10 Mark juxtaposes two stories that give us a picture of what Jesus was talking about in chapter 8 when he said that 'whoever would save his life will lose it, but whoever loses his life for my sake and the gospel's will save it' (8:35). Before drawing our time in Mark to a close, then, we shall reflect briefly on Mark 10.

James and John, the sons of Zebedee, show us what it means to seek to save one's life. Bartimaeus shows us what it looks like to lose one's life. Both portrayals are depicted in terms of seeing and blindness.

Three blind men

Mark 10 closes with two accounts. The first is of James and John coming to Jesus to ask for the two vaunted seats of honor at Jesus' right and left when he reigns in glory as the enthroned king (10:35-45). The second is of blind Bartimaeus, who importunately cries out for mercy from Jesus and, heedless of the crowd's attempts to silence him, is healed (10:46-52).

> And James and John, the sons of Zebedee, came up to him and said to him, 'Teacher, we want you to do for us whatever we ask of you.' And he said to them, 'What do you want me to do for you?' And they said to him, 'Grant us to sit, one at your right hand and one at your left, in your glory.' Jesus said to them, 'You do not know what you are asking. Are you able to drink the cup that I drink, or to be baptized with the

baptism with which I am baptized?' And they said to him, 'We are able.' And Jesus said to them, 'The cup that I drink you will drink, and with the baptism with which I am baptized, you will be baptized, but to sit at my right hand or at my left is not mine to grant, but it is for those for whom it has been prepared.' And when the ten heard it, they began to be indignant at James and John. And Jesus called them to him and said to them, 'You know that those who are considered rulers of the Gentiles lord it over them, and their great ones exercise authority over them. But it shall not be so among you. But whoever would be great among you must be your servant, and whoever would be first among you must be slave of all. For even the Son of Man came not to be served but to serve, and to give his life as a ransom for many.'

And they came to Jericho. And as he was leaving Jericho with his disciples and a great crowd, Bartimaeus, a blind beggar, the son of Timaeus, was sitting by the roadside. And when he heard that it was Jesus of Nazareth, he began to cry out and say, 'Jesus, Son of David, have mercy on me!' And many rebuked him, telling him to be silent. But he cried out all the more, 'Son of David, have mercy on me!' And Jesus stopped and said, 'Call him.' And they called the blind man, saying to him, 'Take heart. Get up; he is calling you.' And throwing off his cloak, he sprang up and came to Jesus. And Jesus said to him, 'What do you want me to do for you?' And the blind man said to him, 'Rabbi, let me recover my sight.' And Jesus said to him, 'Go your way; your faith has made you well.' And immediately he recovered his sight and followed him on the way (10:35-52).

Notice the parallels between the two accounts — James and John on the one hand, Bartimaeus on the other. In both cases: first, Jesus is confronted with a request (10:35, 47-48); second, Jesus initially responds by asking, 'What do you want me to do for you?' (10:36, 51); and third, the parties making the request clearly understand who Jesus is, prompting them to lay before him their true heart's desire (10:37, 47-48).

A fourth parallel exists that is more subtle, underneath the surface of the narrative: in both cases the party making the request is suffering from blindness.

This emerges when we view the differences between the two accounts. Jesus asks the sons of Zebedee and also Bartimaeus, 'What do you want me to do for you?' Yet James and John request glory; Bartimaeus requests mercy. James and John thought they deserved honor and received a 'no' from Jesus. Bartimaeus knew he deserved nothing and received a 'yes' from Jesus. James and John came with a sense of entitlement; Bartimaeus — whose very name meant 'son of uncleanness' or 'son of filth' — with a sense of unworthiness.[68]

---

68. Kenneth E. Bailey, *The Cross and the Prodigal: Luke 15 through the Eyes of Middle Eastern Peasants* (Downers Grove, Ill.: InterVarsity, rev. ed., 2005), p.55.

James and John, while physically seeing, were spiritually blind. They did not realize that the way to be great was to be the servant of all. Bartimaeus, on the other hand, while physically blind, was spiritually seeing. His deepest desire was not the glamorous honors Jesus could provide in the coming kingdom, but Jesus himself.

All three men were blind. Only Bartimaeus knew it.

The following table clarifies the difference.

JAMES AND JOHN (10:35-45)	BARTIMAEUS (10:46-52)
Physically seeing	*Physically blind*
Ask for glory.	Asks for mercy.
Spiritually blind	*Spiritually seeing*
Request based on (inaccurately) perceived strength: 'We are able' (10:39).	Request based on (accurately) perceived weakness: 'Have mercy on me!' (10:47).
Prompted by pride	*Prompted by humility*
Act sneakily — in Matthew's account, the mother of the two brothers speaks for them (Matt. 20:20).	Acts openly: 'throwing off his cloak, he sprang up and came to Jesus' (10:50).
Avoiding the observation of others, coming without the other ten disciples	*Heedless of human perception*
Request comes from insiders.	Request comes from an outsider.
Foster alienation (10:41)	*Fosters unity (10:52)*

The strange way in which naturally blind human beings like you and me receive sight is simply by asking for mercy. That insistent impulse that erupts from deep within to secure glory, to be established as Jesus' right-hand man or woman, is blindness. For it mistakenly listens to the voice within that tells us that the way to save our life is to save it, that the way to become great is to pursue greatness.

Our eyes are opened to the folly of this way of thinking as we acknowledge our true need and do nothing but ask Jesus for mercy. All it takes is an admission of personal blindness. This is clear in another place that deals with blindness, this time in John's Gospel. The Pharisees are incredulous at Jesus' suggestion that they were blind. Jesus responds: 'If you were blind, you would have no guilt; but now that you say, "We see," your guilt remains' (John 9:41).[69] The only thing that stops up Jesus' mercy from flowing into the lives of blind sinners is stubborn denial of blindness.

In the early twentieth century the London newspaper *The Times* invited a small number of nationally respected authors, including G. K. Chesterton, to weigh in with their answers to the question: 'What's wrong with the world?' The result was a series of essays pontificating on who was to blame for the state of the world at the time. Chesterton's contribution read:

---

69. On the blindness/vision motif of John 9:39-41, see Luther, *Luther's Works*, vol. 51, p.37; see also Andreas J. Köstenberger, *A Theology of John's Gospel and Letters* (Biblical Theology of the New Testament; Grand Rapids: Zondervan, 2009), pp.166, 224-25.

Dear Sirs,

I am.

Sincerely yours,

G. K. Chesterton[70]

Blinded on our behalf

Chesterton understood the powerful natural reflex to exonerate self and indict others. The gospel turns this on its head, freeing us to point the finger of indictment back at ourselves — a self-accusation that, paradoxically, is the only way out from underneath the only accusation that really matters. For the great and wonderful surprise of Jesus' mission is that the one person who ever truly deserved to be exonerated at the end of his life allowed himself to be indicted so that you and I can be exonerated at no cost to ourselves.

But surely this is too fraudulently easy? How is this just and right? How can glory-craving, blinded sinners like us receive sight so easily, with nothing but a cry for mercy?

The answer is the primary reason that Mark wrote his Gospel and the very thing announced by Jesus three times in Mark 8 – 10. The king took a criminal's punishment. The lion was treated like a lamb. 'It was wonderful [i.e. full of wonder],' writes Edwards, 'that the Son of God should be

---

70. Cited in Marva J. Dawn, 'Not *What*, but *Who* is the Matter with Preaching?' in *What's the Matter with Preaching Today?*, ed. Mike Graves (Louisville: Westminster, John Knox, 2004), p.75.

arraigned as a criminal.'[71] A battered and bloodied Messiah, so out of sync with what hopeful Jews anticipated in their coming king — and with what you and I expect in a Savior — is at the very heart of Mark's Gospel. It was little exaggeration for German scholar Martin Kähler, drawing on Mark 8:27 — 9:13, to call the Gospels 'passion narratives with extended introductions'.[72]

The great glory of the Christian gospel is that Mark's Gospel does not end at chapter 8. The blindness of Bartimaeus, the blindness of the disciples, and the blindness in you and me is accounted for. For Jesus died. And that is a far bigger deal than how our mutual funds are doing, or who is leading the nation we live in, or global warming, or lost jobs, or diseases that we may contract, or struggling marriages. No matter what happens economically, or politically, or in our jobs, health, or relationships, in the days ahead, the most fundamental reality of our existence stands — unchanged, unmoved, gloriously open, inviting nothing more than a 'yes'. For Jesus, deserving a 'yes', received a 'no', so that we, deserving a 'no', can receive a 'yes'.

Perhaps the best one-verse summary of Mark is 10:45, nestled in between the two closing accounts of Mark 10 considered above, where Jesus gives the foundation beneath the call for his disciples to serve one another: 'For even the

---

71. Jonathan Edwards, 'Annotations on Passages of the Bible,' in *Selections from the Unpublished Writings of Jonathan Edwards* (ed. Alexander B. Grosart; Edinburgh, 1865), p.140.
72. Martin Kähler, *The So-Called Historical Jesus and the Historic, Biblical Christ*, trans. Carl E. Braaten (Philadelphia: Fortress, 1964), p.80.

Son of Man came not to be served but to serve, and to give his life as a ransom for many.' The gospel of grace is not about what we can do for God, but about what God has done for us in Jesus Christ. 'If you have anything of your own,' preached Spurgeon, 'you must leave it all before you come. If there is anything good in you, you cannot trust Christ.'[73] All we bring is our need. All we bring is our blindness.

For Jesus Christ, the consummate king, was, in the deepest sense, 'seeing'. He was the only person never to have been morally blinded by sin. Yet in the suffering predicted throughout the second half of Mark, Jesus allowed himself to become 'blind' so that you and I, blind sinners, can have our sight restored. Jesus' 20/20 vision is given to us. Our sight is restored by acknowledging our moral blindness and asking for mercy. Nothing more is required for his accomplishment, his vision, his victory, his life, to wash over us in a flood of grace. This is surprising grace.

Jesus asked the sons of Zebedee, 'What do you want me to do for you?'

He asked Bartimaeus, 'What do you want me to do for you?'

But most crucially he asked this question a third time, to his own Father (see Matt. 26:39; Luke 22:42; John 5:19; 8:28).

James and John asked Jesus for glory. Bartimaeus asked Jesus for mercy. God the Father asked Jesus to lay down his life, securing both glory *and* mercy for those who admit their blindness and cling to Christ.

---

73. Charles Spurgeon, *Faith* (New Kensington, Pa.: Whitaker House, reprinted 1995), p.35.

PART 3 – LUKE:

THE SURPRISE OF

OUTSIDERS AS INSIDERS

7.

JESUS' SURPRISING
COMMUNITY

IN AN ADDRESS given in 1944 to young men at the
University of London, C. S. Lewis reflected on the universal
human desire to be *included*. He called the object of this
mysterious craving the 'inner ring'.

'I believe,' he said, 'that in all men's lives at certain periods,
and in many men's lives at all periods between infancy and
extreme old age, one of the most dominant elements is the
desire to be inside the local ring and the terror of being left
outside.'[74] This inner ring offers 'the delicious knowledge
that we … are the people who *know*'.[75] After all, 'The world
seems full of "insides", full of delightful intimacies and

74. C. S. Lewis, 'The Inner Ring,' *The Weight of Glory and Other Addresses*,
pp.110-11. Lewis was addressing young male students in this lecture, so
we will leave his gender-specific language alone. His remarks transcend
gender boundaries, of course.
75. *Ibid.*, p.111; emphasis original.

confidentialities.'[76] And the inveterate lust to be on the inside of these confidentialities is 'skilful in making a man who is not yet a very bad man do very bad things'.[77] A desire simply to be on the inside — whatever that inside may be — is a powerful motivator that propels us in all sorts of ways and generates a host of different sins. A desire to be an insider may lead to stealing if the inner ring is wealthy; to sensuality if the inner ring is promiscuous; to cheating if the inner ring is academically superior; or to legalism if the inner ring is bound by rules and regulations. 'It is tiring and unhealthy to lose your Saturday afternoons,' remarks Lewis, 'but to have them free because you don't matter, that is much worse.'[78]

Jesus' community turns the ring inside out

Lewis is tapping into one of the strongest drives we experience as fallen human beings, one of the clearest and most powerful ways our brokenness engages with the social and relational world in which we are daily immersed. It is so natural to our broken intuitions that it feels normal, like fish in water. We long to be included, even if — or, *especially* if — that means that others are excluded. We deeply desire to be 'in'.

Luke, more than any other Gospel, addresses this. In Matthew, as we have seen, Jesus' *definition of morality* is counterintuitive, the reverse of what we would expect, as he castigates the morally scrupulous rather than the morally

---

76. *Ibid.*, p.118.
77. *Ibid.*, p.116.
78. *Ibid.*, p.112.

profane. In Mark, Jesus' *mission* is counterintuitive, as the King of all kings is treated as the criminal of all criminals. In Luke we find that Jesus' *community* is counterintuitive. Those whom one would expect to be 'in' are excluded, and those whom one would expect to be 'out' are included. The inner ring is inverted.[79]

The dynamic here is similar to that of Matthew, yet Matthew highlights a moral question, Luke a social one. The two are by no means mutually exclusive. But what we emphasized in Matthew is mainly a vertical issue; what we are focusing on in Luke is mainly a horizontal issue. In Matthew we saw the human desire to be 'in' with respect to God; in Luke we see the desire to be 'in' with respect to other people.

Once more we go to a single extended passage as a window into the whole Gospel. In doing so we find that Luke surprises us with the way Jesus turns all our social intuitions upside down. Once more, we are confronted with a deeply surprising Jesus Christ.

Luke's pervasive social reversals

The sting of exclusion and the craving for inclusion are universal. C. S. Lewis knew it, and Luke knew it. The representative passage we will look at is Luke 1:5-38. Here we find that the deepest twist of Luke is that Jesus includes the

---

79. On this theme in Luke, see also John R. W. Stott, *Basic Introduction to the New Testament* (Grand Rapids: Eerdmans, 1964), pp.30-37; Jeremias, *Rediscovering the Parables*, p.179; I. Howard Marshall, *Luke: Historian and Theologian* (Downers Grove, Ill.: InterVarsity, 3rd edition, 1988), p.141.

outsiders and excludes the insiders. Though to some degree this social reversal is seen in all four Gospel accounts, it is most central to Luke. In setting things up this way we do not mean to say that Jesus does not want those who are already naturally 'insiders' to likewise be included; his deepest heart is that they be included too. But their own social advantages make it harder for them to see their need for Jesus and his gospel.

Before moving to Luke 1, let's briefly take stock of the rest of his Gospel to clarify just how pervasive a theme this is.

In Luke 2, it is lowly shepherds who are those highlighted as noteworthy visitors to the newborn Jesus (2:8-20) — not, as in Matthew's Gospel, the wise men from the east who were important enough to drop in to the king's palace on their way to Bethlehem (Matt. 2:1-7). Shepherds were *not* at the top of the social ladder in the first century. One rabbinic tradition lumped shepherds together with tax collectors and revenue farmers as those who will have a particularly hard time repenting before God and making restitution to others, in the light of the notorious lack of integrity with which their job was carried out.[80] New Testament scholar Joachim Jeremias writes of first-century shepherds that, 'Most of the time they were dishonest and thieving; they led their herds on to other people's land.'[81] Yet these socially marginalized men were given a front-row seat in witnessing the incarnation of the Son of God.

---

80. Babylonian Talmud, *Baba Qamma* 94b; quoted in Bailey, *Jesus through Middle Eastern Eyes*, p.183.

81. Joachim Jeremias, *Jerusalem in the Time of Jesus*, trans. F. H. Cave and C. H. Cave (London: SCM, 1969), p.305.

The rest of Luke's Gospel continues similarly. Though we cannot dwell on every instance, a snapshot from each chapter of the social inversions that permeate Luke will give a representative sense of how pervasive this motif is. As we do so, we bear in mind the deeply ingrained social hierarchies built into the fabric of the New Testament world concerning men and women, Jew and Gentile, educated and ignorant, rich and poor, free and slave, upright and immoral, political zealots and political collaborators. Their day was as authoritarian, structured, and hierarchical as today's Western society is egalitarian, equal-opportunity-oriented, and 'liberated'.

In Luke 3, it is those of direct descent from Abraham who are designated by John the Baptist as a 'brood of vipers' to be replaced, if need be, by the very stones underfoot (3:7-9). In Luke 4, Jesus outrages his hearers by reminding them that two of the ultimate Jewish insiders, Elijah and Elisha, healed not the Israelites, but the outsiders of the day — a poor Gentile widow and a diseased pagan soldier named Naaman (4:25-27). In chapter 5, Jesus invites a tax collector named Levi to become an insider, and then eats with him at his house while those Jewish men with the best education, the best pedigree and the highest moral standards grumble (5:27-32). Jesus blesses outsiders and curses insiders in Luke 6, blessing the poor, the weeping, and the reviled, while pronouncing woes on the rich, the laughing, and those about whom others speak well (6:20-26).

Showing that he does not have a kind of reverse bias

against insiders simply because they are insiders, Jesus accepts a dinner invitation from a Pharisee named Simon in chapter 7, just as he had eaten with a tax collector in chapter 5. The same pattern of embracing outsiders surfaces once more, however, as a socially alienated woman — 'a woman of the city, who was a sinner' (7:37) — is welcomed and forgiven, while Simon appears to be left on the outside, failing to understand the debt for which he himself needs forgiveness (7:36-50). In Luke 8, Jesus dubs the common crowd his 'mother' and 'brothers', leaving his actual mother and brothers outside (8:19-21; see also 11:27-28).[82]

In Luke 9, a young child is picked up by Jesus and placed among the disciples as an example of whom they should receive, while those who are ready to leave everything behind — so long as they can first say goodbye to their parents — are not 'fit for the kingdom of God' (9:46-48, 62). In chapter 10, a socially despised Samaritan is the hero of the famous parable, rather than the socially revered priest or Levite (10:25-37).[83] And in Luke 11, Jesus says the men of Nineveh — outsiders if ever there were any — will rise

---

82. Kenneth Bailey notes the significance of Jesus including women in this identification of his disciples: 'In our Middle Eastern cultural context, a speaker who gestures to a crowd of *men* can say, "Here are my brother and uncle and cousin." He *cannot* say, "Here are my brother and sister and mother" ' (Bailey, *Jesus through Middle Eastern Eyes*, p.192; emphases in the original).

83. Samaritans, inhabitants of the small region south of Galilee and north of Judea, were considered half-breeds as they were descendants of the Jews who had stayed behind and intermarried with Gentiles during the exiles.

up and condemn the crowds listening so attentively to him (11:29-32). Chapter 12 describes the rejection of a rich man, contrasted with the abundant treasures belonging to those who sell their possessions and give to the needy (12:13-21, 31-34).[84]

In Luke 13, many will expect to get into the kingdom of God, yet be excluded, while 'people will come from east and west, and from north and south' — from outside — 'and recline at table in the kingdom of God' (13:25-29, 34-35). In Luke 14, the insiders who are initially invited to the great banquet end up rejected, replaced by 'the poor and crippled and blind and lame' (14:15-24). The younger son in Luke 15, who wishes his father dead and wastes his inheritance, is 'in', while the older son, working hard all his life, appears to be 'out' (15:11-32) — a commentary on those who are listening: the tax collectors and sinners on the one hand, and the Pharisees and scribes on the other (15:1-2).

In chapter 16, it is poor, wretched Lazarus who enters heaven while his rich neighbor is tormented in hell (16:19-31). In Luke 17, it is only the despised Samaritan who returns to express gratitude to Jesus among the ten lepers who are healed (17:11-19), and in chapter 18, it is the hated tax collector who goes home justified, not the ethically scrupulous and socially exalted Pharisee (18:9-14). In chapter 19, Jesus eats with and saves the oppressor, Zacchaeus the tax collector

---

84. Here we remember the divine blessing that was presumed by ancient Jews to rest on those whom God had prospered in material terms.

(19:1-10). Luke 20 describes the transfer of a 'vineyard', an Old Testament symbol for the people of God, to 'other' (Gentile) tenants (20:9-18), and Luke 21 praises the offering of a poverty-stricken woman instead of the gifts of the rich (21:1-4). In Luke 22, we find ourselves at the final week of Jesus' life.

The great biblical reversal

Scattered throughout the accounts highlighted here are many more of Jesus welcoming the socially alienated and alienating the socially revered. We have mentioned a representative few. All through Luke, outsiders are in and insiders are out. Tax collectors, prostitutes, Gentiles, Samaritans, children, 'sinners', younger sons: 'in'. Teachers of the law, scribes, Pharisees, lawyers, the dutifully religious, the socially respected, older sons: 'out'. Several scholars appropriately suggest that Luke 19:10 should be seen as a one-verse summary of Luke's Gospel: 'For the Son of Man came to seek and to save the lost.'[85] Paul Tournier puts it well: 'There indeed is a reversal — God prefers the poor, the weak, the despised. What religious people have ... difficulty in admitting, is that He prefers sinners to the righteous.'[86]

In today's terms, Jesus came to seek and to save sex workers, pimps, dishonest corporate leaders, welfare dependents, convicted felons, crooked journalists, drug

---

85. For example, Marshall, *Luke: Historian and Theologian*, p.116; Blomberg, *Jesus and the Gospels*, p.165.
86. Tournier, *Guilt and Grace*, p.114.

addicts, disenfranchised ethnic minorities, social rejects, the homeless, the smelly, the disgusting.[87]

Tournier calls this 'the great biblical reversal'.[88] The glad heart of God is drawn to those whom the world holds at arm's length. This socially upending theme of Luke is not unique to the third Gospel. Not only the other Gospels but the whole Bible, both explicitly and implicitly, consistently deconstructs the social hierarchies that make qualitative judgments about people and put them in their place on the basis of birth and accomplishment. In one rabbinic prayer, for example, a Jewish man would thank God that he was neither a Gentile nor a slave nor a woman. Explicitly, these three are the very barriers Paul breaks down in Galatians 3:28: in Christ Jesus, 'There is neither Jew nor Greek, there is neither slave nor free, there is neither male nor female.' Implicitly, these are the three categories into which those who made up the core group of the church plant at Philippi in Acts 16 fall — the Gentile Philippian jailer, a slave girl whose demon is exorcised and Lydia the businesswoman.

The inclusion of outsiders is uniquely evident, however, in the third Gospel. We turn now to Luke 1.

Angelic appearances to Zechariah and Mary

Once more we begin with the relevant passage. Unlike our

---

87. This can be seen particularly clearly in noting those with whom Jesus ate — on which see Craig L. Blomberg, *Contagious Holiness: Jesus' Meals with Sinners* (NSBT 19; Downers Grove, Ill.: InterVarsity, 2005).
88. Tournier, *Guilt and Grace*, p.122.

representative passages in Matthew and Mark, here we go right to the start of the Gospel where we will see how it is the outsider who is commended, while the insider is rebuked — the outsider is in, and the insider is out.

After explaining in the first four verses *what* he has written ('an orderly account' of 'the things that have been accomplished among us'), *for whom* he has written ('Theophilus'), and *why* he has written ('that you may have certainty'), Luke describes two successive appearances by the angel Gabriel. The first is to Zechariah, father of John the Baptist. The second is to Mary, mother of Jesus:

> In the days of Herod, king of Judea, there was a priest named Zechariah, of the division of Abijah. And he had a wife from the daughters of Aaron, and her name was Elizabeth. And they were both righteous before God, walking blamelessly in all the commandments and statutes of the Lord. But they had no child, because Elizabeth was barren, and both were advanced in years.
>
> Now while he was serving as priest before God when his division was on duty, according to the custom of the priesthood, he was chosen by lot to enter the temple of the Lord and burn incense. And the whole multitude of the people were praying outside at the hour of incense. And there appeared to him an angel of the Lord standing on the right side of the altar of incense. And Zechariah was troubled when he saw him, and fear fell upon him. But the angel said to him,

'Do not be afraid, Zechariah, for your prayer has been heard, and your wife Elizabeth will bear you a son, and you shall call his name John. And you will have joy and gladness, and many will rejoice at his birth, for he will be great before the Lord. And he must not drink wine or strong drink, and he will be filled with the Holy Spirit, even from his mother's womb. And he will turn many of the children of Israel to the Lord their God, and he will go before him in the spirit and power of Elijah, to turn the hearts of the fathers to the children, and the disobedient to the wisdom of the just, to make ready for the Lord a people prepared.'

And Zechariah said to the angel, 'How shall I know this? For I am an old man, and my wife is advanced in years.' And the angel answered him, 'I am Gabriel, who stands in the presence of God, and I was sent to speak to you and to bring you this good news. And behold, you will be silent and unable to speak until the day that these things take place, because you did not believe my words, which will be fulfilled in their time.' And the people were waiting for Zechariah, and they were wondering at his delay in the temple. And when he came out, he was unable to speak to them, and they realized that he had seen a vision in the temple. And he kept making signs to them and remained mute…

In the sixth month the angel Gabriel was sent from God to a city of Galilee named Nazareth, to a virgin betrothed to a man whose name was Joseph, of the house of David. And the virgin's name was Mary. And he came to her and said, 'Greetings, O favored one, the Lord is with you!' But she was greatly troubled at the saying, and tried to discern what sort of greeting this might be. And the angel said to her, 'Do not be afraid, Mary, for you have found favor with God. And behold, you will conceive in your womb and bear a son, and you shall call his name Jesus. He will be great and will be called the Son of the Most High. And the Lord God will give to him the throne of his father David, and he will reign over the house of Jacob forever, and of his kingdom there will be no end.'

And Mary said to the angel, 'How will this be, since I am a virgin?'

And the angel answered her, 'The Holy Spirit will come upon you, and the power of the Most High will overshadow you; therefore the child to be born will be called holy — the Son of God. And behold, your relative Elizabeth in her old age has also conceived a son, and this is the sixth month with her who was called barren. For nothing will be impossible with God.' And Mary said, 'Behold, I am the servant of the Lord; let it be to me according to your word.' And the angel departed from her (1:5-22, 26-38).

It is clear from the way Luke opens his Gospel account that he is setting up a deliberate contrast between Zechariah and

Mary. As with our study of James and John versus Bartimaeus in Mark 10, we can see this by noting what is similar between the two accounts and what is different.

The similarities

What is similar between the way Luke describes what happens to Mary and to Zechariah?

Several things stand out. Both are visited by the angel Gabriel. Both are 'troubled' by this visit (1:12, 29). Both are assured and told by the angel not to be afraid. Both are informed of a son soon to be born to them, and are told what to name him. Both are told that 'he will be great' (1:15, 32) and that he will have a special, divinely ordained role to play in the ongoing story of redemption, particularly with respect to the fate of Israel (1:16, 32-33). Both Zechariah and Mary later exult with a poem of praise to the Lord (1:46-55, 68-79). Finally, both question this angelic announcement — and each with good reason!

This last similarity is puzzling, even contradictory. For even though both express doubt, Zechariah is rebuked and disciplined, while Mary is commended and reassured. How is it that Zechariah's doubt results in his temporary loss of the ability to speak, while Mary suffers no such punishment? Three observations help us here:

- First, Zechariah and Mary did not say exactly the same thing. Zechariah asked, 'How shall I know this?' (1:18) — literally, 'According to what will I know this?' Mary asked, 'How will this be?' (1:34). Zechariah's response was a

121

request for proof, as though the angel's word from the Lord was not enough. Mary's response was quiet wonder.

- Secondly, we can simply take Gabriel's response to be indicative of what was going on inside the heart of Zechariah and of Mary. We do not need to be told the precise nature of the doubt that each expressed in order to perceive what Gabriel's response to the questions expressed by Zechariah and Mary indicated about the state of the heart of each.

- Thirdly, we are told explicitly later in the narrative that Zechariah lacked faith and that Mary possessed faith. In verse 20, Gabriel explains that Zechariah's punishment was 'because you did not believe my words'. In verse 45, on the other hand, Zechariah's wife Elizabeth greets Mary with the words: 'blessed is she who believed'.[89]

While both Mary and Zechariah express doubt, then, the way each expression is articulated indicates a deep difference of heart-posture. For Zechariah, doubt prevailed over belief. For Mary, belief prevailed over doubt. This brings us to consider what other differences appear between the two accounts.

Roles reversed

The differences that would have made Zechariah socially favored are many. He was a male, while Mary was a female — a distinction that carried far greater social weight in that

89. I am grateful to Tyler Kenney for pointing out this third distinction to me.

culture than in the West today. Zechariah was old, while Mary was young, perhaps just barely into her teenage years. He was a priest, a member of the religious elite, while she was just one of the common people. Zechariah was financially stable in his role as a priest — in much the same way that a government worker in some nations today is funded by tax revenue, Jewish priests were supported by a portion of the revenue brought in by the people's offerings. That's pretty good job stability — as long as people carry on sinning, you will have food to eat! Mary, on the other hand, was poor, as evidenced by her bringing just two doves for her sacrifice — an allowance for those who could not afford a lamb (2:24; cf. Lev. 12:8). Zechariah was not only married, but had married a woman who was also from the revered line of Aaron (1:5), while Mary was betrothed but not yet married, in a day when marriage afforded women significant social stability.

Zechariah, we are told, not only had just the right social pedigree, but he and his wife were also 'both righteous before God, walking blamelessly in all the commandments and statutes of the Lord' (1:6). Perhaps Mary was similarly righteous, but this is nowhere stated explicitly. One other difference strikes us. The angel's prediction of an imminent pregnancy for Zechariah's wife Elizabeth was cause for rejoicing. We know from Luke 1:13 that Zechariah had evidently been praying for a son for some time. For Mary, on the other hand, an unmarried teen, an illegitimate pregnancy would be a public disgrace.

All this leads us to expect a certain response from Zechariah and a certain response from Mary. With everything going in Zechariah's favor, one would expect his reaction to Gabriel's announcement to be immediate, explosive, and one of faith-filled joy. And with everything going against Mary, one would expect her response to be as *faithless* as Zechariah's would be *faithful*.

Yet here we come to the most surprising difference of all. Zechariah's response was faithless; Mary's was faith-filled. Zechariah asked for proof and was struck dumb; Mary meekly submitted and was commended.

The roles ought to have been exactly reversed. Zechariah, the insider, responds in the way that Mary, the outsider, ought to have responded. Mary, the outsider, responds in the way that Zechariah, the insider, ought to have responded.

Zechariah was not, it would appear, ultimately rejected. He did, after a period of muteness, recover his voice and his faith, following through on the angel's order that the baby should be named John. Yet we are still struck with how they initially responded. And isn't this, after all, the truest test of what is inside us? Isn't what first pops out of us when a trial washes over us the truest indicator of the actual state of our hearts — the way we react *before* we have time to catch ourselves and pass our response through the filter of how we want others to perceive us? As C. S. Lewis put it, 'If there are rats in a cellar you are most likely to see them if you go in very suddenly. But the suddenness does not create the rats; it only prevents them from hiding.'[90]

90. C. S. Lewis, *Mere Christianity* (New York: HarperCollins, 2001), p.192.

The first chapter of Luke strikes a note that will resound through the whole Gospel. The same surprise we see in the *ministry* of Jesus all through Luke — that outsiders are in and insiders are out — is seen right from the start in the *birth* of Jesus. Not only what he does in the world, but how he comes into the world is fraught with surprise.

8.

HONEST SINNERS

'JESUS COMES FOR sinners,' writes Brennan Manning, 'for those as outcast as tax collectors and for those caught up in squalid choices and failed dreams. He comes for corporate executives, street people, superstars, farmers, hookers, addicts, IRS agents, AIDS victims, and even used-car salesmen.'[91]

No social prerequisites required

Some of us today have grown up with tremendous privilege: long-standing participation in the church, perhaps going back several generations; pastors or other Christian leaders in the extended family; respect in the community; a life immersed in the teaching of the Bible; conversion at a young age.

Others of us have no transparent claim to be a member of the people of God, if social prerequisites are a factor.

---

91. Brennan Manning, *The Ragamuffin Gospel* (Colorado Springs: Multnomah, 2005), p.23.

We are not particularly intelligent, or dynamic, or clever, or impressive. Perhaps we came to Christ late in life. The world of the Bible largely remains a foreign universe to us.

The Gospel of Luke has something to say to both groups. To the insiders among us Luke says, 'Your superior social position is a gift from God. Steward it well. But be careful — not only are the privileges you were born with not beneficial to your standing in the people of God, they may be detrimental' (cf. Phil. 3:7). For it is easy, so easy, to allow inherent blessings of ancestry, birth, and name subtly to build a false sense of entitlement.

To the outsiders among us Luke says, 'Your inferior social position is no impediment at all to your standing in the people of God. No social prerequisites are required. You are most welcome.'

The most inclusive exclusivism of all

Jesus' radical inversion of social mores in Luke is both extreme inclusivism and extreme exclusivism at the same time. Jesus presents us with a third way that is neither what the culture tells us nor what religion tells us.

Our current culture in the West stands for inclusivism. Everyone should be included. No exclusion.

Most religion stands for exclusivism. There is exclusion all right — and it is for those who don't measure up to that religion's standards.

Put differently, the culture tells us that there are no

outsiders.[92] Religion, on the other hand, certainly endorses a division between the outsiders and the insiders, and says that the outsiders are those who do not measure up in some way.

Jesus presents us with a third way of understanding exclusivity and inclusivity, the outsiders and the insiders. Jesus shows us the strictest of exclusivism and the widest of inclusivism *at the same time*, united in the same person — in himself. Only through him can one enter the kingdom. This is radically exclusive. Yet anyone can come. This is radically inclusive.

Freed for authentic community

Because this grace is open to all — *all* — the gospel of grace provides the only resource for authentic community. Here we remember that the craving for community is not only for extroverts. It is for humans. Introverts, too, need community. The hunger for fellowship is rooted in the image of God, not in our personal wiring.

The very essence of Christianity is help, acknowledgement of inability, salvation through the work of another, admission of guilt. Yet we Christians are a strange bunch. Somehow we allow ourselves to slide into a 'good enough',

92. This is often said, however, in a way that turns those who affirm the existence of outsiders into being outsiders themselves. This is a tolerance of everything but intolerance. It is inclusive of everything but exclusivity. The claim to universal inclusiveness is itself exclusive. It is a claim to possess the very knowledge that its proponents say we cannot have. To say that one cannot diagnose outsiders, on the grounds that such diagnosis arrogantly claims a transcendent knowledge of ultimate reality, in itself involves a claim to transcendency and therefore cuts its own feet from under it.

'minimum standard' social culture that frenetically strives to keep up appearances. In his book *Forgotten God*, Francis Chan writes:

A while back a former gang member came to our church. He was heavily tattooed and rough around the edges, but he was curious to see what church was like. He had a relationship with Jesus and seemed to get fairly involved with the church. After a few months, I found out the guy was no longer coming to the church. When asked why he didn't come any more, he gave the following explanation: 'I had the wrong idea of what church was going to be like. When I joined the church, I thought it was going to be like joining a gang. You see, in the gangs we weren't just nice to each other once a week — we were family.'[93]

It is sobering to consider that many of our churches — and let's be honest, we ourselves are far more often the problem than the solution — foster a more domesticated brand of community than a gang. Real fellowship is elusive. Even among our fellow brothers and sisters in Christ, we wear masks, and hide sins, and parade virtues, and judge others. Many find the church to be the place where it is hardest, not easiest, to speak openly about personal struggles.

---

93. Francis Chan, *Forgotten God: Reversing our Tragic Neglect of the Holy Spirit* (Colorado Springs: David C. Cook, 2009), p.152. See also Manning, *Ragamuffin Gospel*, pp.16, 56-57.

This is deeply ironic and tragic because in the Christian gospel we have the one resource that can unlock the heart and free us to take off the masks. As long as we view the Christian church as a club for those who make the grade socially, we will be unwilling to speak freely of our shortcomings as believers. Only when the single prerequisite to inclusion in the church is joint agreement that there is no prerequisite will we let down our guard. The Gospel of Luke takes us there.

The fundamental distinction between churches is not that some of them have sinners and others do not. The fundamental distinction is that some churches have *honest* sinners and other churches have *self-protecting* sinners. The question is not whether we are sinful or not, but whether or not we are honest about it. James 5:16 was not written to a segment of the church but to all members: 'Confess your sins to one another and pray for one another, that you may be healed.'

This is not to say that the horizontal dimension of the Christian life should be allowed to crowd out the vertical. The church community must, we remember, find its nourishment not ultimately in one another, but in sustaining a vital connection to the vine. Christians are called to fix their eyes on God in Christ as the one with whom they are in deepest and most meaningful fellowship. Yet even this supports, rather than detracts from, fellowship with one another. The call to love God and the call to love one another are not in competition; they are mutually reinforcing. But the order is critical: put the vertical first, and you get the horizontal with it; put the horizontal first, and you get neither. A. W. Tozer explains why:

> Has it ever occurred to you that one hundred pianos all tuned to the same fork are automatically tuned to each other? They are of one accord by being tuned, not to each other, but to another standard to which each one must individually bow. So one hundred worshipers met together, each one looking away to Christ, are in heart nearer to each other than they could possibly be were they to become 'unity' conscious and turn their eyes away from God to strive for closer fellowship.[94]

Putting fellowship with one another above fellowship with God destroys both.

But even here we have not yet penetrated to the foundational key to real Christian community. To this key, in conclusion, we turn.

Welcomed inside once and for all

The surprise of Luke that outsiders are 'in' and insiders are 'out' funnels down into one central and all-important realization. In Christ we are, in the only sense that matters, *in*.

Apart from the gospel, we crave to be 'in', yet we never can be. In the gospel this craving is calmed as we are, once and for all, on the inside. The puffed-up mystique of the 'inner ring'

---

94. A. W. Tozer, *The Pursuit of God: The Human Thirst for the Divine* (Camp Hill, Penn.: Christian, 1982), p.80.

has been deflated. The itch for meaningful inclusion has been satisfied. Those pining after the 'inner ring' must get in if they are to feel worth anything, and they generally fail to do so. The gospel turns both these miseries on their head. We no longer have to be in — and we *are* in.

We must see therefore that, for all our talk in this chapter (and in the church today) about 'community', we will only be spinning our wheels without going anywhere if we disconnect the cultivation of community from the gospel. We see this in Galatians 2, an account of a disruption of real community by none other than the apostle Peter: 'Before certain men came from James, he was eating with the Gentiles; but when they came he drew back and separated himself, fearing the circumcision party' (Gal. 2:12). Fellowship was broken.

Now how does Paul handle this? Certainly, he rebukes Peter: 'I opposed him to his face' (Gal. 2:11). Yet how does Paul do this? What is his diagnosis? Does he remind Peter that Christians are not supposed to be racist? Does he encourage Peter to get up earlier and spend more time reading Scripture? Does he tell Peter that this is poor evangelistic strategy? Does Paul remind Peter that Christians are to be loving towards all, even outsiders? Any of these responses would have been legitimate. But Paul goes to the root of the problem. He identifies Peter's error as *gospel* error. 'I saw that their conduct was not in step with the truth of the gospel,' says Paul (Gal. 2:14). What was Peter's mistake? Evidently he was not believing the truth of the gospel in all its richness. But *in what way* was Peter not believing the gospel? The text tells us he was: 'fearing the circumcision party' (Gal. 2:12).

Fear — that was what drove Peter. Here is the point: the gospel liberates us not only from fear of the judgment of God in the future, but also from fear of the judgment of men in the present.

For in Christ, we are already 'in'. The craving to be welcomed in, affirmed, brought inside, declared okay — *justified* — has been met. Remember, it is immediately on the heels of this passage in Galatians 2 that Paul pens the most famous words in the whole Bible on justification by faith (Gal. 2:16). Peter was not simply being racist. He was losing his grip on justification.

In Leo Tolstoy's 1869 novel *War and Peace*, a story of early nineteenth-century Russia under threat of invasion by Napoleon, an unimpressive second lieutenant named Boris Drubetskoi searches out the socially significant Prince Andrei. Requesting the prince's whereabouts from other officers, Boris receives only condescending snubs. Entering a room, Boris discovers Prince Andrei impatiently listening to an older, much-decorated Russian general who wants desperately to win Andrei's attention and favor. The prince is finding himself bored with this over-eager general and, noticing Boris, promptly leaves the general and sidles over to Boris for a more enjoyable chat. Tolstoy writes:

> Boris at this instant clearly understood what he had suspected before, that in the army there was, above

and beyond the fact of subordination and discipline as laid down in the code, and which they in the regiments knew by heart, and which he knew as well as anyone else — there was another still more essential form of subordination, one which compelled this anxious general with the purple face to bide his time respectfully, while Captain Prince Andrei, for his own satisfaction, found it more interesting to talk with Ensign Drubetskoi. More than ever Boris decided henceforth not to act in accordance with the written law, but with this unwritten code.[95]

It does not require military experience to know first-hand exactly what Tolstoy describes. This 'unwritten code' offers acceptance, welcome, approval. This approval is intoxicating when extended, and crushing when refused.

In the gospel of grace, the power that this unwritten code exerts on all of us is unmasked and exposed in all its fraudulence. For we are already, and apart from any social prerequisite we bring to the table, in.

---

95. Leo Tolstoy, *War and Peace*, trans. Nathan H. Dole (New York: Crowell, 4 vols., 1932), vol. 1, p.301.

9.

THE ONLY KEY

BUT HOW? HOW can it be that outsiders can *freely* become insiders?

The ultimate insider

The answer is hinted at in Luke 9:51 — Jesus 'set his face to go to Jerusalem'. What did he do when he got there? As Hebrews puts it, Jesus went 'outside the camp' (Heb. 13:11-13). Again and again in the Old Testament, a member of God's people is forced to spend time outside the camp on account of ritual uncleanness (for example, Lev. 13:46; 14:8; Num. 5:3; Deut. 23:12). Jesus became unclean, however, *for us*. He went outside the camp so that you and I, who are unclean outsiders, can immediately gain access inside — inside the only inner ring that matters: favor with God, the fellowship of Eden restored. Forgiveness. *Shalom*.

The key to experiencing the inside of all insides, contrary to what we would expect, lies outside of us. Evangelical leader

Al Mohler writes that Christians tend to 'believe that their major problem is something that has happened to them, and that their solution is to be found within. In other words, they believe that they have an alien problem that is to be resolved with an inner solution. What the gospel says, however, is that we have an inner problem that demands an alien solution.'[96] Our culture tells us that the problem is outside us and the solution is inside us. The gospel tells us that the problem is inside us and the solution is outside us.

Nowhere is this more powerfully depicted than in the account in Luke 5 of the healing of the paralyzed man lowered by his audacious friends through a roof. Jesus' immediate solution is: 'Your sins are forgiven' (5:20).

What if the next time you found yourself at the doctor's office, he looked at your charts and then turned to you and said, 'Don't worry — your sins are forgiven!' Aside from the question of how the doctor is able to have the authority to forgive sins — a problem the Pharisees had with Jesus in this passage — we would be perplexed because the doctor would be responding to a physical problem with a moral solution.

The paralytic's friends thought, 'We bring you a paralytic. We're here for a physical solution, not a moral one. Forgiveness is nice, but that's not the problem!'

And Jesus says, 'Yes, it is.'

The friends thought, 'We brought him here to be healed!'

And Jesus says, 'Exactly.'

96. R. Albert Mohler Jr., 'Preaching with the Culture in View,' in Mark Dever *et al.*, *Preaching the Cross* (Wheaton, Ill.: Crossway, 2007), p.81.

The moral problem is the problem beneath the problem. It's the crisis behind every crisis. The paralytic and his friends thought, quite naturally, that the greatest dilemma in the paralytic's life was his physical paralysis. But Jesus treated first the more fundamental dilemma: spiritual paralysis. The paralytic thought his problem was something that had happened to him. In truth, his problem was him. It was not circumstantial but spiritual; not the events of his life but the state of his soul. Just a few verses later, Jesus explicitly speaks of spiritual poverty as a sickness: 'Those who are well have no need of a physician, but those who are sick. I have not come to call the righteous but sinners to repentance' (5:31-32).

But how was this fundamental problem resolved? By forgiveness, yes. But how was forgiveness won? By what right was Jesus able to offer not only physical healing but ultimate healing to the paralytic?

In this way: on the cross, the one true insider became an outsider so that you and I, naturally born outsiders, can freely be brought in.

C. S. Lewis closed his address 'The Inner Ring' with a stirring warning not to fall prey to the lust to be inside the inner ring: 'Unless you take measures to prevent it, this desire is going to be one of the chief motives of your life, from the first day on which you enter your profession until the day when you are too old to care.'[97] Wise words, words to be heeded. But Lewis, for all his helpfulness in diagnosing this pervasive sickness, failed to provide the medicine. The

97. Lewis, 'The Inner Ring,' p.114.

key 'measure to prevent' the fierce desire to be an insider is to abide in the truth that the one person who truly was an insider became an outsider in order to bring us in.

We could put it in terms of biblical theology, viewing the Bible through the lens of its united storyline culminating in Christ. In our first parents, Adam and Eve, we fell and were kicked outside the Garden of Eden. We have been outsiders ever since. Noah and his family were saved by being inside the ark, while the rest of the world perished outside. In Exodus, God's people were delivered only to find themselves outside, in the wilderness. Joshua and Judges tell the painful story of Israel trying to get inside the promised land. In the exile, God's people were once again taken outside the land. And so on.

Genesis 3 onwards, in other words, tells the story of humanity *trying to get back in*, and of God's merciful provision of a tabernacle and then a temple — a place to meet with God, a place to be *entered*. Even this, however, was off limits to all but a handful of specially designated priests.

Then Jesus came on the scene. He announced that *he* was the temple (John 2:18-22). The apostles later explained that those who are united to Christ become living stones in a temple of which Christ is the cornerstone (1 Peter 2:4-6; cf. 1 Cor. 6:19). Those who are in Christ have become, in the most important sense, insiders. And in the new earth the remaining corruption that still plagues us with feelings of being condemned outsiders will vanish: 'And I saw no temple in the city, for its temple is the Lord God the Almighty and the Lamb' (Rev. 21:22-27).

Hell is filled with people who believe they deserve to be outside hell and inside heaven. Heaven is filled with people who believe they deserve to be outside heaven and inside hell.[98] One more way we are surprised by Jesus.

Know that you shouldn't be in. Look to Christ. Be at rest. You are in.

---

98. I owe this sentence to a sermon preached on 13 June 2010 by Ray Ortlund at Immanuel Church in Nashville, Tennesee, USA. A similar statement can be found in D. Martyn Lloyd-Jones, *The Cross: God's Way of Salvation* (Wheaton, Ill.: Crossway, 1986), p.75.

PART 4 – JOHN:
THE SURPRISE OF THE
CREATOR AS A CREATURE

10.

JESUS AND TRUE IDENTITY

'THE INCARNATION OF Christ is a most extraordinary and amazing affair,' wrote the Puritan John Gill. 'It is wonderful indeed, that the eternal Son of God should become man; that he should be born of a pure virgin … and all this in order to effect the most wonderful work that ever was done in the world, the redemption and salvation of men: it is a most mysterious thing, incomprehensible by men.'[99]

This incomprehensible event is the surprise that lies at the heart of the fourth Gospel. In Matthew, we have seen the surprise of disobedient obedience; in Mark, the surprise of the king as a criminal; and in Luke, the surprise of the outsiders as insiders. In John, we come to the surprise of the Creator as a creature. Jesus' *identity* is counterintuitive.

---

99. John Gill, *A Body of Doctrinal Divinity* (Paris, Ark.: The Baptist Standard Bearer, reprinted 2004), p.378.

Here we are not asking, as in Matthew, what obedience looks like; nor, as in Mark, what Jesus came to do; nor, as in Luke, who comprises his community. We are asking *who he is*.

As with previous chapters, we will focus on a particular passage as a window into the whole Gospel account. That passage will be the first eighteen verses of John 1. Here we find that the Word becoming flesh is indeed 'a most extraordinary and amazing affair' — one more example of the way the real Jesus surprises us into wonder and freedom.

Echoes of Genesis

Way back at the beginning of the Bible, the book of Genesis opens with the words, 'In the beginning...' (Gen. 1:1), and goes on to describe how the spoken word of God brought all things into existence (cf. Ps. 33:6, 9; 2 Peter 3:5). That first chapter of the Bible speaks of creation, light and darkness, and life out of empty nothingness. And in the ensuing narrative, God's creation rejects its own Creator.

All this is true of the first chapter of John's Gospel as well. 'Genesis 1 described God's first creation,' writes Bible scholar Leon Morris; 'John's theme is God's new creation.'[100] Of special importance is the way Genesis 1 describes creation by the 'word' of God. For John 1 takes the very categories and conceptual world of Genesis to describe Jesus himself as

---

100. Leon Morris, *The Gospel According to John* (NICNT; Grand Rapids: Eerdmans, rev. ed., 1995), p.65.

the 'Word' (*Logos*) of God.[101] In Genesis we find the one God speaking: time and again we read, 'And God said...' In John we find a surprising identification of this word by which God brought all things into existence.

And at the pinnacle of this exalted introductory prologue to his Gospel, John inserts the most astonishing statement, one that seems blatantly irreconcilable with the first creation account of Genesis 1: 'And the Word became flesh' (1:14).

We begin once more by reproducing the relevant passage. Throughout the rest of this chapter we will give special attention to verse 14.

In the beginning was the Word, and the Word was with God, and the Word was God. He was in the beginning with God. All things were made through him, and without him was not any thing made that was made. In him was life, and the life was the light of men. The light shines in the darkness, and the darkness has not overcome it.

There was a man sent from God, whose name was John. He came as a witness, to bear witness about the light, that all might believe through him. He was not the light, but came to bear witness about the light.

101. See Sidney Greidanus, *Preaching Christ from Genesis: Foundations for Expository Sermons* (Grand Rapids: Eerdmans, 2007), pp.6, 51-52; Andreas J. Köstenberger, *A Theology of John's Gospel and Letters* (Biblical Theology of the New Testament; Grand Rapids: Zondervan, 2009), pp.178-79, 337-41; Vern Poythress, *In the Beginning Was the Word: Language — A God-Centered Approach* (Wheaton, Ill.: Crossway, 2009), pp.12, 19-21, 45-46.

The true light, which enlightens everyone, was coming into the world. He was in the world, and the world was made through him, yet the world did not know him. He came to his own, and his own people did not receive him. But to all who did receive him, who believed in his name, he gave the right to become children of God, who were born, not of blood nor of the will of the flesh nor of the will of man, but of God.

And the Word became flesh and dwelt among us, and we have seen his glory, glory as of the only Son from the Father, full of grace and truth. (John bore witness about him, and cried out, 'This was he of whom I said, "He who comes after me ranks before me, because he was before me."') And from his fullness we have all received, grace upon grace. For the law was given through Moses; grace and truth came through Jesus Christ. No one has ever seen God; the only God, who is at the Father's side, he has made him known (1:1-18).

Overturning deeply entrenched beliefs

Before directly tackling this passage we must be clear about two important beliefs built into the ancient world out of which John wrote. One has to do with the Greek world of John's day, and the other with the Jewish world.[102] With these on the table

---

102. Scholars have long debated which of these two social milieus is more integral to John's Gospel. Without becoming involved in the debate, all that it is necessary for us to note here is that both were, to some degree, informing John's writing — a balance well maintained by Köstenberger, *Theology of John's Gospel and Letters*, p.338.

we will more clearly see what was so shocking about what John says in the first chapter of his Gospel.

First, we must understand that the *Greek* mind of the day viewed human personhood as deeply dichotomized, or dualistic. By 'dualism' I do not mean *cosmic* dualism — the idea that two equal and opposite forces in the universe, one good and one evil, incessantly war against one another. Rather, I mean *anthropological* dualism, the idea that the human person is essentially two components, body and spirit. The Greek mind of the first century was the recipient of a long and venerable train of philosophical thought going back to Plato which viewed humans as having a physical part (the body) that was inferior and a non-physical part (the soul) that was superior.

Second, we must understand that the *Jewish* mind of the day viewed God the Creator, Yahweh, as utterly transcendent. He was considered to be totally above created matter, wholly other, sovereign, and set apart. At the heart of the Jewish confession was the *Shema*: 'Hear, O Israel: The Lord our God, the Lord is one' (Deut. 6:4).[103] God is one and unique, utterly transcending all created matter, including humans, who have been made in his image: 'I am God and not a man, the Holy One' (Hosea 11:9). This God is incomparably *other*.

The Greeks placed a strong antithesis between soul and body; the Jews placed a strong antithesis between God and humanity. In both cases the material is inferior to the immaterial.

---

103. 'Shema' is a transliteration of the first word of Deuteronomy 6:4: '*Hear*'.

What is the surprise in John's Gospel? The surprise is that the book opens by turning upside down the most basic commitment of both Greek and Jewish thought.

Shocking the Greeks

To the Greek world, John says, 'The Word became flesh.' The Greek term used here is *logos*, and referred in Greek thinking to Reason with a capital 'R', the great organizing principle of the universe, the impersonal rationality behind all that happens, that which injects coherence and stability into the universe.[104] Remember that, to the Greek way of thinking, the corporeal was inherently inferior. Plato taught that death released the human soul from its miserable captivity in a fleshly body, setting the soul free. The Greek mind could no more conceive of the Logos becoming flesh than of the wind becoming mud.

An incarnate Logos was therefore utterly foreign to the Greeks. Yet, as Leon Morris says, 'In one short, shattering expression John unveils the great idea at the heart of Christianity.'[105] For this is precisely what happened. That which brought all things into existence at the beginning of time took on flesh and blood.

Jesus was not a superhuman. Though he was without sin, he was not somehow a semi-divine being. He was a man. The

---

104. See Murray Rae, 'The Testimony of Works in the Christology of John's Gospel,' in *The Gospel of John and Christian Theology*, ed. Richard Bauckham and Carl Mosser (Grand Rapids: Eerdmans, 2008), p.302.
105. Morris, *The Gospel According to John*, p.91.

orthodox Christian doctrine that Christ was both fully God and fully man does not mean that he hovered somewhere between the two — it means that he was fully *both*. As the letter to the Hebrews puts it, Jesus was 'made like his brothers in every respect' (Heb. 2:17).[106]

The Logos became the one thing which, by definition, the Logos could not become. How could the Logos of the universe have a digestive tract? A personality? A certain height and weight? Flesh? D. A. Carson explains the weight of verse 14:

If [John] had said only that the eternal Word assumed manhood or adopted the form of a body, the reader steeped in the popular dualism of the Hellenistic world might have missed the point. But John is unambiguous, almost shocking in the expressions he uses: *the Word became flesh.*[107]

John is not just differing from the dominant Greek thought pattern of the day; John reverses this thought pattern. The Greeks wished to shed the flesh and fly up to heaven; John says that heaven put on flesh and came down to earth.

---

106. Outside of the apostle John's writings, Hebrews is the place in the New Testament that most clearly depicts Jesus' eternal pre-existence with God, as God, combined with his utter humanity (see, for example, Heb. 1:1-3 combined with 2:14-18); see Richard Bauckham, *Jesus and the God of Israel*, pp.233-53.

107. D. A. Carson, *The Gospel according to John* (PNTC; Grand Rapids: Eerdmans, 1991), p.126, emphasis in the original.

Shocking the Jews

That 'the Word became flesh' was no less scandalous to the Jewish world of the day. For, to the Jewish way of thinking, John says, 'This fleshly man was himself somehow Yahweh.' The Word, according to verse 1, 'was with God' — indeed, the Word 'was God'. And it was this divine Word that took on flesh.

The transcendent one, the only being in the universe who cannot be lumped together with any other being, became one of us. The Creator became a creature. The one who molded the clay became an earthen vessel. The Author of history wrote himself into the story.

As with the Greeks, there was a long and cherished tradition in Judaism concerning the 'word' of God. 'By the word of the Lord the heavens were made,' wrote the psalmist. 'For he spoke, and it came to be' (Ps. 33:6, 9). God's word was the mighty divine agent through which the omnipotence of God's creative power erupted.

It would therefore elicit little more than a yawn from his Jewish readers for John to say in John 1:1 that at the beginning of all things, 'The Word was with God, and the Word was God.' The Word was distinct from God ('the Word was with God'), and yet the Word was also included in the very identity of God ('the Word was God'). This Word was the means by which God created the heavens and the earth and was, with God, utterly distinct from the creation.

That this Word would become *flesh* is the scandal of all scandals.

Consider the way the Jewish mind related the Word of God and human flesh is seen in Isaiah 40:

A voice says, 'Cry!'

    And I said, 'What shall I cry?'

All flesh is grass,

    and all its beauty is like the flower of the field.

The grass withers, the flower fades

    when the breath of the LORD blows on it;

    surely the people are grass.

The grass withers, the flower fades,

    but the word of our God will stand forever

(Isa. 40:6-8).

Here we find the same two words, 'flesh' and 'word', that John speaks of in John 1:14.[108] It is striking that in Isaiah human 'flesh' and God's 'word' are set in stark contrast to one another. Flesh falters; the divine word remains forever — absolute antithesis. This was the ancient Jewish way of thinking. God and his word were high, exalted, sovereign, transcendent, sacred.

But in John 1, the two, human flesh and the divine Word, are identified. C. S. Lewis puts it memorably in *Mere Christianity*:

---

108. The Greek version of the Old Testament, the Septuagint, uses the word *rhema*, not *logos*, for the *'word'* of Isaiah 40:8. This ought not to be seen as problematic, however, for 1 Peter 1 quotes Isaiah 40:6, 8 yet uses the two words, *rhema* and *logos*, interchangeably (*logos* in v. 23 and *rhema* in v. 25). Cf. Hengel, 'The Prologue of the Gospel of John as the Gateway to Christological Truth,' in *The Gospel of John and Christian Theology* (ed. Richard Bauckham and Carl Mosser; Grand Rapids: Eerdmans, 2008), p.269, who also notes the language of *'glory'* in both Isaiah 40 and John 1; for example, Isaiah 40:5 speaks of God's *'glory'*, human *'flesh'* and the word that *'the mouth of the Lord has spoken'*.

Among the Jews there suddenly turns up a man who goes about talking as if he was God. He claims to forgive sins. He says he has always existed. He says he is coming to judge the world at the end of time. Now let us get this clear. Among Pantheists, like the Indians, anyone might say that he was a part of God, or one with God: there would be nothing very odd about it. But this man, since he was a Jew, could not mean that kind of God. God, in their language, meant the Being outside the world who had made it and was infinitely different from anything else. And when you have grasped that, you will see that what this man said was, quite simply, the most shocking thing that has ever been uttered by human lips.[109]

The Word tabernacled among us

One way in which the Jewish background to John 1 is reinforced is the verb John chooses to use in verse 14. He says, 'The Word became flesh and dwelt among us.' The term used here for 'dwelt' is the verb form of the Greek noun *skene*, meaning 'tent' or 'tabernacle'. One scholar translates the verb here as 'encamped'.[110] Readers of John's Gospel familiar with

---

109. C. S. Lewis, *Mere Christianity*, p.55. For a dated but helpful discussion of both the Greek and the Jewish backgrounds to the logos of John 1, see Oscar Cullmann, *The Christology of the New Testament*, trans. Shirley C. Guthrie and Charles A. M. Hall (London: SCM, rev. ed., 1963), pp.249-69.
110. J. Ramsey Michaels, *The Gospel of John* (NICNT; Grand Rapids: Eerdmans, 2010), p.74.

the Old Testament would immediately think of the portable temple, the tabernacle, that was transported wherever they went in the wilderness in the course of Israel's wanderings between Egypt and the promised land.

What was the tabernacle? What was the point of this temple?

Unlike some other elements of Jewish faith, such as monotheism, temple worship was not unique to Judaism. Virtually every ancient religion had a temple of some kind. The temple, for Judaism as well as for other religions, was a physical location, a building, where the immortal met the mortal. Here the supernatural and natural collided. The eternal and temporal intersected. The temple was where the divine and the fleshly could temporarily meet — never to mix (lest the profane contaminate the sacred), but rather to come into brief contact with one another.

But at the center of human history, the divine and the fleshly, the supernatural and the natural, *did* mix: 'And the Word became flesh and tabernacled among us.'

Running right through the Old Testament was the development of the theme of the presence of God among his people, a presence restricted to the most sacred of Jewish places — the tabernacle and then the temple. It was here that God dwelt among his people (Exod. 25:8). It was here that glory rested. Fellowship with God was restored, if only for a few moments.

In fact, the tabernacle was a miniature, representative Garden of Eden — complete with sky-blue ceiling and a lampstand decorated like a flourishing tree.[111] The Hebrew word that corresponds to the Greek word *skene* was *shekan*, from which we get our language of Shekinah, the 'glory' of God that became so terrifyingly palpable in the temple.[112] This helps make sense of what John then says in the rest of verse 14: 'And the Word became flesh and dwelt [literally, "tabernacled"] among us, and we have seen his glory.'

In 1 Kings 8:27, Solomon offered a prayer of dedication for the newly built temple, wondering aloud at the absurd notion that an earthly building could contain the God of the heavens: 'But will God indeed dwell on the earth? Behold, heaven and the highest heaven cannot contain you; how much less this house that I have built!'

Will God indeed dwell on the earth? Yes.

Jonathan Edwards reflected on this verse in a handwritten note in the margin of his Bible which expressed the following thought:

> If it was a thing so very wonderful in Solomon's eyes, such a marvelous instance of condescension for God to dwell on earth in the manner he did in the tabernacle

---

111. See Tremper Longman III, *How to Read Exodus* (Downers Grove, Ill.: InterVarsity, 2009), pp.163-64. For a fascinating and developed study of the presence of God throughout the Bible, including an argument that Eden was the original 'temple' that was to be spread over the entire face of the earth, see G. K. Beale, *The Temple and the Church's Mission: A Biblical Theology of the Dwelling Place of God* (New Studies in Biblical Theology 17; Downers Grove, Ill.: InterVarsity, 2004).
112. See discussion in Carson, *John*, pp.127-28.

and temple, how much a greater and more wonderful thing was it for him to dwell with us as our Immanuel in the manner that he did in the human nature of Christ.[113]

In the Old Testament, the supernatural collided with the natural in a physical *building*, where, with severely *limited* access, humans could meet with God in his glory. In the New Testament, the supernatural collided with the natural in a physical *body*, where, with *unlimited* access, humans could meet with God in his glory.

We no longer enter into a temple of wood and stone to meet with God. God has entered into a temple of flesh and blood to meet with us.

Contagious holiness

A crucial distinction between the Old Testament temple, seen in a building, and the New Testament temple, seen in Jesus, is this: the Old Testament temple *repelled* the sick, deformed and unclean; the New Testament temple *attracted* the sick, deformed and unclean. In the Old Testament we read:

Then Haggai said, 'If someone who is unclean by contact with a dead body touches any of these, does it become unclean?' The priests answered and said, 'It does become unclean.' Then Haggai answered and

113. Jonathan Edwards, *The Blank Bible*, in *The Works of Jonathan Edwards*, vol. 24, ed. Stephen J. Stein (New Haven: Yale University Press, 1972), p.378.

said, 'So is it with this people, and with this nation
before me, declares the LORD, and so with every work
of their hands. And what they offer there is unclean'
(Hag. 2:13-14).

In the New Testament we find something very different:

And a leper came to him, imploring him, and kneeling
said to him, 'If you will, you can make me clean.'
Moved with pity, he stretched out his hand and
touched him and said to him, 'I will; be clean.' And
immediately the leprosy left him, and he was made
clean (Mark 1:40-42; cf. Lev. 13).

Jesus upends the moral mathematics we had come to expect
from the Old Testament. In the Old Testament, clean plus
unclean equaled unclean. In the New Testament, clean plus
unclean equals clean. In the Old Testament, defilement is
contagious. In the New Testament, holiness is contagious
(note also 1 Cor. 7:14).[114]

Jesus brought in his train a whole new way of thinking,
a new mental universe in which we do not see ourselves as
basically clean and in danger of defilement, but as basically
defiled and in need of cleansing. Nuzzling up next to Jesus,
we get it.

When Jesus arrived on the scene, he brought a new world
of solid grace, the grace of God that was always there in the

114. See Craig L. Blomberg, *Contagious Holiness*.

Old Testament but was muted, fuzzy, hazy, opaque. Calvin describes the Old Testament as the 'shadows' and the New Testament as the 'substance'.[115] Jesus Christ brought concrete, sharply defined, clearly contoured lines to that real but opaque Old Testament grace. There he stood — right there before us, a flesh-and-blood man, Emmanuel.

The Word became flesh — full of grace and truth; solid, substantive. The law came through Moses; grace and truth came through Jesus.

---

115. John Calvin, *Institutes of the Christian Religion*, ed. John T. McNeill; trans. Ford Lewis Battles (Louisville: Westminster John Knox, 1960), 2.11.114; see also 4.14.25; 4.20.5.

11.

DELIGHT IN THE TRUTH OF EMMANUEL

THE WORD BECAME flesh. Have you ever really stopped and mentally climbed inside this claim? This is too wonderful for words.

It is easy to grow overly familiar with the incarnation. But the fact that the God of heaven became one of us is trivialized if we consign it to little more than a warm devotional thought at Christmas time. Let this extraordinary tenet of orthodoxy sink in afresh.

Myth became fact

In his fascinating essay 'Is Theology Poetry?' C. S. Lewis spoke of the incarnation as 'the humiliation of myth into fact, of God into Man'. He wrote that 'What is everywhere and always, imageless and incffable, only to be glimpsed in dream and symbol and the acted poetry of ritual becomes small, solid — no bigger than a man who can lie asleep in a rowing boat on the Lake of Galilee.'[116] The Word, the Logos, the central meaning of the universe, the integrative center to reality, the climax and culmination of all of human history, that which summoned solar systems into instant existence — at just the right time (Gal. 4:4) — became a helpless baby. The night Christ was born in Bethlehem, writes Chesterton, 'The hands that had made the sun and stars were too small to reach the huge heads of the cattle.'[117]

All that you and I experience, Jesus experienced — with the exception of sin.[118] Indeed, to question whether Jesus led a normal life as we do is to put the whole point back to front. His was the only normal life the world has ever seen. We are the abnormal ones. When Jesus performed miracles he was not doing violence to the natural order. He was restoring the natural order to the way it was meant to be. Blind people were supposed to see. Lame people were meant to walk. Demons did not belong in people. Unlike Adam, who failed to exorcise Satan from the garden when he should have done, Jesus did what Adam ought to have done, exorcising demons from men and women created in God's image. Jesus' miracles were not supernatural. They were truly natural. This fallen world is

---

116. C. S. Lewis, 'Is Theology Poetry?', in *The Weight of Glory and Other Addresses*, pp.99-100.

117. G. K. Chesterton, *The Everlasting Man* (Radford, Va.: Wilder, 2008), p.105.

118. See B. B. Warfield, 'The Emotional Life of Our Lord,' in *The Person and Work of Christ* (Philadelphia: Presbyterian & Reformed, 1950), pp.93-145.

sub-natural. Jesus is the one truly human being who ever lived. The incarnation doesn't give us a hypothetical picture of how we would be able to live if only we were divine. It gives us an actual picture of how we are meant to live, and one day will live, when we are once again fully human.[119]

This is unfathomable. It is not a point of doctrine to download mentally and then move on. We do not master this, like a multiplication table. It is a point to be chewed on and digested. It is to be wondered at. The Word became flesh — not 'the Word created flesh', though that is true. The Word *became* flesh.

This was another portable temple, though this time not carried around by the priests but on his own two legs. This calls for meditation. This calls for worship.

The great prerequisite

The incarnation is not only worthy of our wonder, but foundational to our theology. It is the great prerequisite to every other facet of Christian salvation.[120] There is no crucifixion without incarnation first. There is no resurrection without incarnation first. There is no Second Coming of Christ if there is not a first coming. There is no imputation without the incarnation, for Jesus came as the second Adam, undoing what Adam had done (disobedience) and doing what Adam failed to

---

119. See Jürgen Moltmann, *The Way of Jesus Christ*, trans. M. Kohl (Minneapolis: Fortress, 1993), pp.98-99.
120. See Warfield's comments along these lines in Fred G. Zaspel, *The Theology of B. B. Warfield: A Systematic Summary* (Wheaton: Crossway, 2010), pp.560-67.

do (obedience). In becoming man the Son of God leapt from the safety of heaven and plunged into the world to save his drowning people (Phil. 2:6-11). The incarnation therefore has human sin as its instigation, divine love as its motivation, the Holy Spirit as its cause (in the virgin birth), revelation as its content, redemption as its goal, and worship as its result.

Athanasius, the great fourth-century defender of orthodoxy, spoke of Christ's taking on flesh this way:

> He descended that he might raise us up, he went down to corruption, that corruption might put on immortality, he became weak for us, that we might rise with power, he descended to death, that he might bestow on us immortality, and give life to the dead. Finally, he became man, that we who die as men might live again, and that death should no more reign over us.[121]

This is the surprise of John. The Creator became a creature so that we creatures can be restored to our Creator.

Such grace defies our categories. Moderate grace would have said, 'I'll meet you halfway. I'll grant you a ladder and give you strength to climb it. I'll help you become what you were meant to be.'

God's rich grace said, 'I'll become what you were meant to be.'

---

121. Athanasius, 'Festal Letter,' 10:8; quoted in Thomas G. Weinandy, *Athanasius: A Theological Introduction* (Aldershot: Ashgate, 2007), p.96; cf. p.123.

Entering into history

One important implication of the incarnation, as it is expressed in John 1, is the crucial significance of *history* as we read the Bible.

To everyday readers of the Gospels, as well as to scholars who write about the Gospels, John is often seen as more 'theological' and less historical than the other Gospels. John seems to write an account of Jesus that is more ethereal, more abstract, less rooted in concrete history.

But in John 1:14 we read that the Word became flesh. The Word *entered into history*. That which was with God in the beginning — that which *was* God — entered our time and space. This does not mean that John's Gospel is not theological. It means that the theology we find in John has embedded within it a historical sensitivity. New Testament scholar Richard Bauckham argues this powerfully when he draws on John 1:14 to point out that John's theology itself has a built-in concern for history. Even if we focus only on the theology of John, we are confronted with a radically robust view of time-and-space history.[122] The eternal entered into the temporal. That which is outside of history — the one who created and oversees history — entered *into* history. The richly theological concern of the fourth Gospel is not in tension with a historical concern; the two rise and fall together.

The testimony of John to Jesus Christ is not a testimony rooted in ecstatic visions, lofty self-generated ideals, human

---

122. Richard Bauckham, *The Testimony of the Beloved Disciple: Narrative, History, and Theology in the Gospel of John* (Grand Rapids: Baker, 2007), p.14.

traditions, or subjective impressions. John's testimony is rooted in eyewitness accounts of real events on this planet of this solar system. As John put it in the opening to his first letter, it was a testimony based on that 'which we have heard, which we have seen with our eyes, which we looked upon and have touched with our hands' (1 John 1:1). Here once again John speaks of 'that which was from the beginning' and 'the word [*logos*] of life' (1 John 1:1). The one who entered into history was none other than the very Word of God, eternally one with God.

The fact that the Christian faith is robustly historical is not simply an important sidelight on it; the historicity of our faith is integral to the faith itself. Subtract historicity and the Christian faith topples. Consider the bodily resurrection of Christ. In 1 Corinthians 15, Paul says that if Jesus did not walk out of the tomb in real flesh, we are still in our sins. The historical mediates the spiritual. What happens in heaven when we stand before God, forgiven, is grounded in what happened in space and time on this earth. The two are not alternatives; they are bound up with one another.

The portrait of Jesus in the Gospels is unmitigatedly historical. Often John's Gospel is the one that is viewed as the least tethered to history. In fact its very theology, a theology of the Word becoming flesh, contains implanted within it a deep concern for historical accuracy. One way we see John's concern to give thoughtful expression to his Gospel account is the meticulous care with which this account is crafted. Bauckham has shown, for instance, that John's prologue (1:1-18) and epilogue (21:1-25) are meant to provide clear bookends to the Gospel, since the Greek text of the prologue contains 496 syllables and the epilogue 496 words. Bauckham notes that 496 is mathematically special as it is both a perfect number and a triangular number. He further notes that the two mini purpose statements to John (20:30-31; 21:24-25) each contain forty-three words.[123] The point is that John's Gospel is not the fruit of unthinking, ecstatic, high-flying theologizing, but is a carefully and deliberately crafted account that takes its content very seriously.

Surprising grace is historical grace.

The 'I am'

Once again, as with Matthew, Mark, and Luke, our treatment of a single passage from the Gospel is meant only to be a window into the whole Gospel account. New Testament scholar Martin Hengel points us in this direction when, referring to the first eighteen verses of John's Gospel, he writes:

The climax and goal is the incarnation of the Word in v. 14. It is the key to the twenty-one chapters that follow … the one decisive point that is developed in the whole Gospel has already been made in the four words of v. 14, *ho logos sarx egeneto* ['the Word became flesh'].[124]

123. Richard Bauckham, *Jesus and the Eyewitnesses: The Gospels as Eyewitness Testimony* (Grand Rapids: Eerdmans, 1996), pp.364-66.
124. Martin Hengel, 'The Prologue of the Gospel of John as the Gateway to Christological Truth,' in *The Gospel of John and Christian Theology* (ed. Richard Bauckham and Carl Mosser; Grand Rapids: Eerdmans, 2008), p.268.

We see the subversive grace of God in writing himself into the story of human history throughout the Gospel of John. For example, the shocking wedding of Word and flesh, sacred and profane, supernatural and natural, concludes John's Gospel. In chapter 20, after Jesus' bodily resurrection, Thomas misses out on Jesus' appearance to the other disciples (20:19-23). Skeptical Thomas can hardly believe that Jesus has come back to life and brashly announces that unless he places his finger in the mark where the nails were — unless he sees the *fleshly* reality of Jesus — he will not believe. When Jesus appears and invites Thomas to touch him and see the holes in his scarred hands, Thomas' responds by adding to his discovery of Jesus in the flesh a clear affirmation of Jesus as divine: 'My Lord and my God!' (20:28).

A particularly striking way in which the Word-becoming-flesh motif courses throughout John is that Jesus repeatedly refers to himself using the theologically loaded words, 'I am.'[125]

In Exodus 3, God had revealed himself to Moses with the name 'Yahweh', 'I AM.' When Moses asked God how he should respond when asked by fellow Israelites in Egypt to identify God by name, God responded: ' "I AM WHO I AM." ... Say this to the people of Israel: "I AM has sent me to you" ' (Exod. 3:14). This divine name is also used a total of seven times in Deuteronomy and Isaiah to refer to the utter transcendence

---

125. In what follows I am indebted to Richard Bauckham, *Testimony of the Beloved Disciple*, pp.243-50; Bauckham, *Jesus and the Israel of God*, pp.39-40.

of the God of Israel (Deut. 32:39; Isa 41:4; 43:10, 25; 45:18; 46:4; 51:12).

Throughout John's Gospel, too — drawing on either Exodus, Deuteronomy, or Isaiah, or some combination of the three — we find the divine name used. But here it is on the lips of *Jesus*.

It is often noted that Jesus speaks of himself with an introductory 'I am' seven times throughout John. This is partly true. There are in fact fourteen such instances. Seven of these are obvious and seven are more subtle. The obvious ones we will call the completed 'I am...'s. They are completed in the sense that in each case Jesus states, 'I am the...' (In grammatical terms, the verb is followed by a predicate.) They are:

I am the bread of life (6:35, 41, 48).
I am the light of the world (8:12).
I am the door of the sheep (10:7, 9).
I am the good shepherd (10:11, 14).
I am the resurrection and the life (11:25).
I am the way, and the truth, and the life (14:6).
I am the true vine (15:1).

These seven predicative, or completed, sayings, taken cumulatively, communicate the riches of the new life Jesus brings.

These are only half the occurrences, however. We can call the remaining seven the stand-alone 'I am' sayings. These are more subtle, because they are not explicitly used to introduce a metaphor, as the completed 'I am...'s do. They are:

Jesus said to her, '*I am*, who speaks to you' (4:26).
And he said to them, '*I am*; do not fear' (6:20).
'…if you do not believe that *I am*, you will die in your sins' (8:24).
'When you lift up the Son of Man, then you will know that *I am*' (8:28).
'Truly I say to you, before Abraham was, *I am*' (8:58).
'I say it to you now, before it happens, so that you might believe when it happens that *I am*' (13:19).
Jesus said to them, '*I am*' (18:5; see also 18:6, 8).[126]

A few of these are fairly obvious, such as in John 8:58: 'Before Abraham was, I am.' This instance stands out conspicuously as a clear reference to the great 'I AM' of the Old Testament. The fact that Jesus is here aligning himself with Yahweh is confirmed in the response of the religious authorities: they pick up stones to kill Jesus for uttering blasphemy (8:59). Other stand-alone instances of 'I am', however, are easily missed. Many translations, for example, render 'I am' in John 6:20 and 18:5 as 'It is I.' This disguises the reference to the divine name of Old Testament precedence.

All through John, then, Jesus identifies himself, explicitly and implicitly, with the transcendent God of the Old Testament, Yahweh, 'I AM.' The Creator, John is saying, has taken on creatureliness.

---

126. The translations of these seven stand-alone 'I am' sayings are my own.

Both good and great

Recognizing these two sets of 'I am' sayings is more than a matter of intellectual curiosity. Taken together, these fourteen declarations breathe new life into us.

It is important to see both sets of seven 'I am' sayings in John's Gospel. Not only is the number seven significant in the Bible, indicating completeness and perfection, but both sets of seven 'I am' statements in John provide a crucial piece of encouragement in our understanding of who Jesus is and how he helps us. For the stand-alone uses of 'I am' show us Jesus as God; the completed 'I am...'s show us Jesus as Savior.

In the stand-alone 'I am' sayings Jesus identifies himself as Yahweh. Somehow, in a way that bursts the comfortable bounds of Jewish monotheism, Jesus himself is included in the divine identity. In the completed 'I am...'s, however, while this inclusion in the divine identity is certainly present, the thrust of each statement is what Jesus is for needy sinners: 'I am the bread of life.' 'I am the good shepherd.' 'I am the resurrection and the life.' The stand-alone occurrences of 'I am' exhibit Jesus' greatness. The completed 'I am...'s exhibit his goodness.

A thousand encouraging implications arise out of this union of greatness and goodness, might and mercy, strength and salvation. Take prayer, for example.

When we kneel down to pray, we are coming to one who is both utterly powerful and utterly good. He is both King and Lover, both omnipotent and omni-merciful. He is able to help us, and he is willing to help us. If in our prayers to Christ

we are confident only of the stand-alone 'I am' statements
— confident that he is great but not that he is good — we
would know that he can answer our prayers, but we could
not be sure that he cares enough to respond. If in our prayers
to Christ we are confident only of the completed 'I am...'s
— confident that he means well and loves us and wishes the
best for us, but not that he is able to do much about it —
we would know that he cares for us but might think that he
cannot help much.

In Jesus Christ, believers have a Lord and a Savior. He is
over us and he is next to us. Jesus is a King to represent God to
us as well as a Priest to represent us to God.

12.

DOWN THE LADDER

ONE PROBLEM REMAINS, however. How is it good news that Jesus is both able to save and willing to save *if we are rebels*? His greatness and his goodness are certainly a potent combination. But how does it engage with you and me, in all our sin and failure?

The true ladder

The answer is found in John 1:12: 'But to all who did receive him, who believed in his name, he gave the right to become children of God.' Believing in the name of Jesus, which is an ancient way of saying believing in the person of Jesus, opens up the floodgates for the greatness and goodness of God manifested in Christ to come pouring into my life.

The point is made strikingly at the end of John 1. Here we find a rather strange encounter between Nathanael and Jesus after Philip has persuaded the skeptical Nathanael to come and see whether Jesus really is 'him of whom Moses in the

Law and also the prophets wrote' (1:45). We will pick up the narrative at verse 47:

> Jesus saw Nathanael coming towards him and said of him, 'Behold, an Israelite indeed, in whom there is no deceit!' Nathanael said to him, 'How do you know me?' Jesus answered him, 'Before Philip called you, when you were under the fig tree, I saw you.' Nathanael answered him, 'Rabbi, you are the Son of God! You are the King of Israel!' Jesus answered him, 'Because I said to you, "I saw you under the fig tree," do you believe? You will see greater things than these.' And he said to him, 'Truly, truly, I say to you, you will see heaven opened, and the angels of God ascending and descending on the Son of Man' (1:47-51).

It is the final verse here that is particularly arresting. On learning of Jesus' knowledge that he had spent some time under a fig tree, Nathanael is won over to see that Jesus is indeed 'the Son of God', 'the King of Israel' (1:49). Yet Jesus says that they will behold 'greater things' than this evidence of supernatural knowledge. They will see 'heaven opened, and the angels of God ascending and descending on the Son of Man' (1:51).

Just as astute readers of the Old Testament would have picked up the veiled reference to the tabernacle in John 1:14, so they would have discovered another veiled reference here. In Genesis 28, Isaac sends his son Jacob to find a wife from among his own people. En route, Jacob spends the night at Bethel. 'And he dreamed, and behold, there was a ladder set up on the earth, and the top of it reached to heaven. And behold, the angels of God were ascending and descending on it!' (Gen. 28:12). The Lord goes on to reaffirm to Jacob his great covenant promises to the patriarchs (Gen. 28:13-15).

In Genesis 28, heaven is opened and the angels of God ascend and descend on a ladder that connects heaven and earth. In John, heaven is opened and the angels of God ascend and descend on the Son of Man. What is the point of Jesus' iconic statement in John 1:51?

Jesus is saying, 'I am the ladder. I am the connection between heaven and earth.' Luther was right: 'Christ applies the story of the dear patriarch to Himself: now the angels will ascend and descend on Him as on a ladder.'[127]

Jacob saw a ladder bring heaven to earth. The disciples saw Jesus bring heaven to earth. When Jacob awakes from his strange dream he whispers: 'How awesome is this place! This is none other than the house of God, and this is the gate of heaven' (Gen. 28:17). But while Jacob said in Genesis 28, '*This is the gate of heaven*', Jesus in effect said in John 1, '*I am the gate of heaven*.'[128] Indeed, he would explicitly say as much later in the fourth Gospel (10:7, 9).

---

127. Luther, *Luther's Works*, vol. 22, p.201; see also p.331.

128. Leonard Goppelt, *Typos: The Typological Interpretation of the Old Testament in the New*, trans. Donald H. Madvig (Grand Rapids: Eerdmans, reprinted 1982), p.186; note also Craig S Keener, *The Gospel of John: A Commentary* (Peabody, Mass.: Hendrickson, 2 vols., 2003), vol. 1, p.489.

The ultimate goal of the incarnation

Jesus' greatness and goodness come flooding into our lives, then, because he himself has become the ladder by which heaven is opened to us. We do not climb a ladder of obedience to trigger the mercy of God.

But how did Jesus become the ladder? How did he do this? By going to the cross.

We have been exulting in the incarnation in this chapter. Well, so we should! This is the great surprise of the Gospel of John. The incarnation is not, however, the ultimate focus of John's Gospel. While the incarnation is necessary if Jesus is to be our true ladder to heaven, it is not sufficient. The incarnation was not Christ's ultimate goal any more than donning scuba gear is the ultimate goal of a professional rescue diver. The donning of the wetsuit is for the purpose of saving someone.

The ultimate goal of the incarnation is given to us in the final four chapters of John. The incarnation paved the way for the crucifixion and resurrection. The purpose of the fourth Gospel is not simply to convince us that the Creator became a creature, but that it is by trusting this one who was crucified and raised that we receive eternal life (see 20:30-31). The manger led to the cross, which led to our deliverance. The letter to the Hebrews makes this plain in its own language: 'Since therefore the children share in flesh and blood, he himself likewise partook of the same things [incarnation], that through death [crucifixion] he might destroy the one who has the power of death, that is, the devil, and deliver all those who through fear of death were subject to lifelong slavery [deliverance]' (Heb. 2:14-15).

In John 19 Jesus was crucified. On the cross, Jesus knew 'that all was now finished' (19:28). A short time later he breathed his last with these very words: 'It is finished' (19:30).

Finished!

Buddha's last words were: 'Try to accomplish your aim with diligence.' Christ's last words? 'It is finished.' Buddha left this world exhorting his followers to work hard. Jesus left this world inviting his followers to rest in what had been done for them. Louis Markos describes Buddhism as 'centripetal, turning the self back upon itself', whereas Christianity is 'centrifugal', pointing to a Savior outside of us.[129]

Buddha died giving his followers a ladder to climb. Jesus died becoming for his followers the ladder they could never climb.

He came down to us

We return one final time, then, to the unique glory of the gospel.

Not just Buddhism, but every major world religion, in essence, gives people a ladder to climb to God — rules, guidelines, laws, stipulations. Humans climb up the ladder to God.

Christianity is the only world religion in which God comes down to man. 'The case was certainly desperate,' wrote Calvin, 'if the Godhead itself did not descend to us, it being impossible for us to ascend.'[130]

---

129. Louis Markos, *Apologetics for the Twenty-First Century* (Wheaton, Ill.: Crossway, 2010), p.77.

130. Calvin, *Institutes of the Christian Religion*, 2.12.1.

Other religions say, 'Here is the ladder: climb up it.' The surprising grace of the gospel says, 'God climbed down the ladder for us.' Other religions say, 'Here is the way to walk.' Jesus said, 'I am the way' (14:6). Other religions say, 'Here is how you can be lifted up to God.' Jesus said, 'I will be lifted up, on the cross, for you' (see 3:14; 8:28; 12:32-34). The religious authorities of Jesus' day asked him, 'What must we do, to be doing the works of God?' (6:28). Jesus said, 'This is the work of God, that you believe in him whom he has sent' (6:29). The one crucial work is to trust in the one who was sent to perform your work for you.

In other words — to use the language of John 1:14 — the gospel is the only way to God that combines both grace and truth. In Exodus 34, in perhaps the most significant Old Testament revelation of God's character (Exod. 34:6-7), God's glory, grace, and truth were revealed to Moses. In John 1:14, it is Jesus whose 'glory' is revealed, and it too is 'full of grace and truth'. This is why John says, 'We have seen his glory' (1:14). For Moses God's glory was full of grace and truth in abstraction. In Jesus, God's glory in human form — grace and truth joined together — was not an abstraction but an event, a person. Moses hid his face from God's glory. In Jesus, God's glory was itself given a face.

Why does it matter for us today that Jesus is 'full of grace and truth'? The culture of religious tolerance all around tends to emphasize grace without truth, forgiveness without any real standard that would make forgiveness necessary. World religions tend to emphasize truth without grace, a standard to meet without any sense of someone else having met it on our behalf. But Jesus came full of grace *and* truth.

The great 'I AM' became what we are. 'Christ came down from heaven,' wrote Jonathan Edwards, 'and dwelt among us on the earth; the Word was made flesh and dwelt amongst us, full of grace and truth, that we might partake of his fullness and might be made happy by him and in him.'[131]

The 'I AM' became what we are so that we can become what he is — not divine, but sons of God. The king became a slave so that we slaves can become kings once more, the kings we were made to be (Gen. 1:28). He came down so that we can go up. The Creator became a creature. Martin Luther put it well in a hymn composed in 1531:

'Tis Christ our God, who far on high
Had heard your sad and bitter cry;
Himself will your salvation be,
Himself from sin will make you free.

Welcome to earth, thou noble Guest,
Through whom e'en wicked men are blest!
Thou com'st to share our misery,
What can we render, Lord, to thee![132]

---

131. Jonathan Edwards, *The 'Miscellanies' 501-832* in vol. 18 of Ava Chamberlain, ed., *The Works of Jonathan Edwards* (New Haven: Yale University Press, 2000), p.385.
132. Martin Luther, 'From Heaven Above to Earth I Come,' in *Dr Martin Luther's Deutsche geistliche Lieder* (BiblioLife, 2009), pp.60-61.

CONCLUSION

THE GRACE FLOODING out from Jesus Christ to sinners and sufferers and to no one else is radically subversive of our intuitive expectations and religious sensibilities. Jesus gives grace — he gives *himself* — to the undeserving, and to those who feel themselves to be so.

We have seen this surprising grace in each Gospel account. There is certainly plenty of overlap among the four Gospels. Yet certain emphases rise to the surface as uniquely highlighted in each one.

In Matthew, Jesus exposes externalized obedience as thinly veiled moral rottenness. In Mark, the long-anticipated king takes up the fate of a criminal. Luke shows us Jesus inverting the social assumptions, with insiders ending up outside, and outsiders finding themselves inside. And the great surprise of John is that the eternal God who made all things became flesh and blood.

Jesus defies our sense of fair play with regard to morality, the atonement, the nature of the church, and his incarnation. His message and mission disrupt all our inherent expectations of who he is and how following him works.

We have noted in concluding each chapter, moreover, the foundation for these surprising reversals: Jesus allowed himself to be treated as the undeserving one on our behalf, so that we undeserving sinners can be freely treated as those who are deserving, with nothing more on our part than faith in him. The obedient one suffered for our disobedience. The king suffered for our crimes. The insider suffered for us outsiders. The Creator suffered for us creatures.

Clever Bible scholars sometimes try to drive a wedge between the Christianity presented in the Gospels and the Christianity presented in the letters of Paul. The Gospels, so the allegation goes, give us moral teaching; the letters give us the gospel of grace. Yet such a portrait of the New Testament is forced and unfaithful to what we have seen in the Gospels. These four narratives exude grace — surprising grace, subversive grace.

The purpose of this little book on the Gospels has been to peel away the accretions of attempts to domesticate Jesus and his endless goodness that have accumulated over the years in the hearts of some of us. Jesus Christ simply cannot be tamed. He is not one-dimensional, not predictable; he does not map on to our pre-existing expectations of what he is like. He is wonderfully disruptive. He demands that we surrender our lives to him, holding back nothing, letting go of the functional lifelines of human approval, bank accounts, sexual pleasure, cultivating a reputation — indeed, of all that beckons to provide a more tangible and immediate security. Let him expose these lesser saviors as the frauds they are, letting us down so profoundly after promising so much. Only Jesus, the real Jesus, the surprising Jesus, fills us. And he does so to an overflowing degree. It's simply who he is.

But make no mistake. With Jesus it is all or nothing. He is not asking to be added to our lives. He is asking to uproot our festering anxieties and redirect all our cowering hopes squarely onto himself. Jesus does not medicate us. He renovates us. He is not addition; he is transformation.

Could it be that you and I have been wading in the shallows of fellowship with Christ, thinking we have exhausted the ocean? Could it be that there is more for us to experience in Jesus than we have yet dreamed of?

In his 1950 reflection 'What Are We to Make of Jesus Christ?', C. S. Lewis answers that question by remarking: 'There is no question of what we can make of him; it is entirely a question of what He intends to make of us. You must accept or reject the story.'[133] Lewis then concludes with what is a fitting conclusion to our own study of Jesus and his scandalous grace revealed in the four Gospels. May God in his mercy open the eyes of a rising generation to the wonder of this Christ, and his endless surprises of mercy and grace to those who least deserve it but most desire it.

---

133. C. S. Lewis, 'What Are We to Make of Jesus Christ?' in *God in the Dock: Essays on Theology and Ethics* (Grand Rapids: Eerdmans, 1970), p.160.

Lewis writes:

The things He says are very different from what any other teacher has said. Others say, 'This is the truth about the Universe. This is the way you ought to go,' but He says, '*I* am the Truth, and the Way, and the Life.' He says, 'No man can reach absolute reality, except through Me. Try to retain your own life and you will be inevitably ruined. Give yourself away and you will be saved.'

Jesus Christ says, 'If you are ashamed of Me, if, when you hear this call, you turn the other way, I also will look the other way when I come again as God without disguise. If anything whatever is keeping you from God and from Me, whatever it is, throw it away. If it is your eye, pull it out. If it is your hand, cut it off. If you put yourself first you will be last. Come to Me, everyone who is carrying a heavy load, I will set that right. Your sins, all of them, are wiped out, I can do that. I am Re-birth, I am Life. Eat Me, drink Me, I am your Food. And finally, do not be afraid, I have overcome the whole universe.'[134]

---

134. *Ibid.*

SCRIPTURE INDEX